A gift for: _____

From: _____

Standing on the
Promises

ED YOUNG
COUNTRYMAN

He who promised is faithful.

HEBREWS 10:23

Introduction

These devotional thoughts on God's promises were put together by my friend and brother, fellow pastor and associate, Dr. Wallace Henley. In addition to being an astute theologian, Wallace is an outstanding teacher and proclaimer of God's Word. He has the uncanny ability to take my meanderings from the pulpit and put them into practical thoughts that are easy to understand and apply. Thank you, my friend.

I would be remiss if I did not express my personal appreciation to the Second Baptist Family. Week by week they hear the spoken Word of God and respond faithfully and with great enthusiasm. Thank you, folks, for being such an encouragement to me. Please know I consider it an honor and privilege to serve as your pastor.

Most of all I want to thank my wife, Jo Beth, for standing with me all these years. I have watched so many of God's promises lived out in her life as she has loved and nurtured our children and grandchildren. I hope she will continue discovering His promises for her life as she so beautifully exemplifies a woman of God. I love you, Joby.

And now, thank you for using this book as a tool in your devotional time with the Lord. I pray and believe you will find the strength, resolve, peace, or comfort you need at this very moment in your life. May God bless you as you stand confidently on these, His promises from His Word.

For no matter how many promises God has made, they are "Yes" in Christ.

2 CORINTHIANS 1:20 NIV

January

January 1

*"HE HAS SENT ME TO PROCLAIM RELEASE
TO THE CAPTIVES, AND RECOVERY
OF SIGHT TO THE BLIND, TO SET FREE THOSE
WHO ARE OPPRESSED, TO PROCLAIM
THE FAVORABLE YEAR OF THE LORD."*

LUKE 4:17-19

The four stages of Christian living are illustrated by Israel's passage from Egypt to the Promised Land. "Going out" is leaving the realm of sin and condemnation, and receiving Christ as Savior. "Going through" is journeying through a wilderness of challenge and testing, which produces growth, strength, and obedience. "Going in" is making a decision of serious commitment to the Lordship of Christ. "Going on" is receiving, enjoying, and leaning upon God's promises. Determine this will be a year of God's favor for you, a year of "going on" in His promises.

January 2

I have rejoiced in the way of Your testimonies,
As much as in all riches.

PSALM 119:14

God's covenant is a treasure chest, the riches inside His promises. All can claim God as "Father," Creator. Only those in covenant with Him know God as *Abba*, "Daddy." An individual makes promises to many people, such as bosses, vendors, politicians, and charities. But promises to our own children include our lives, legacies, and fortunes. Throughout this book, I refer to promises to God's "covenant people." You come into this special relationship by receiving God's only begotten Son, Jesus Christ, into your life. Then the chest of treasures with all its riches is yours, in Christ!

*Therefore, do not throw away your confidence,
which has a great reward. For you have need of
endurance, so that when you have done the
will of God, you may receive what was promised.*

HEBREWS 10:35-36

Endurance is the key to accomplishing God's will, leading to the actualization of His promises in your experience. Like David with Goliath, the giants you confront can help you grow in and prove your endurance. Don't run from them, but trust God to give you victory. Also like David, you likely will encounter temptation. In the deep of the night, when no human is watching, your integrity will be tested. Rather than weakening, celebrate the opportunity to endure, thereby accomplishing His will and receiving the blessing of His promise!

January 4

"You did not choose Me but I chose you, and appointed you that you would go and bear fruit, and that your fruit would remain, so that whatever you ask of the Father in My name He may give to you."

JOHN 15:16

If you're married to Jesus, don't sleep with the "flesh," because you may bear its fruit—immorality, impurity, sensuality, idolatry, sorcery, enmities, strife, jealousy, outbursts of anger, disputes, dissensions, factions, envy, drunkenness, and carousing (Galatians 5:19). God promises that intimacy with Him results in the fruit of the Spirit—love, joy, peace, patience, kindness, goodness, faithfulness, gentleness, and self-control (Galatians 5:22–23). He made you and married you to bear His fruit, not that of the illicit lover, the "flesh."

*"Do not worry then, saying, 'What will we eat?'
or 'What will we drink?' or 'What will we wear for
clothing?' For the Gentiles eagerly seek
all these things; for your heavenly Father knows
that you need all these things."*

MATTHEW 6:31-32

Edith suffered Alzheimer's and was in a care facility. For years, her husband, Burt, made daily visits. He brought flowers, whispered in her ear, fed her, fixed her hair, and even learned to give her a facial. "She doesn't know who you are," a nurse said. "Why do you do this?" Burt smiled. "She may not know who I am, but I know who she is. We've been in a covenant a long time, and I'm going to take care of her." The special relationship between God and His redeemed people is a covenant. He's promised to be our Caregiver, even when we may not recognize Him.

> "Of Him all the prophets bear witness that
> through His name everyone who believes in Him
> receives forgiveness of sins."
>
> ACTS 10:43

I heard of a psychotherapist who commented that if all the patients in his institution could understand they were forgiven half the beds would be empty. Another, Karl Menninger, argued that without the concept of personal sin there is no awareness of personal forgiveness, and no real solution to guilt. The promise of forgiveness is twofold. We are to receive God's forgiveness personally, then extend our forgiveness to those who've wronged us. That's when we truly receive the promise of the forgiveness of sins.

January 7

*Just as it is written, "BEHOLD, I LAY IN ZION
A STONE OF STUMBLING AND A ROCK
OF OFFENSE, AND HE WHO BELIEVES IN HIM
WILL NOT BE DISAPPOINTED."*

ROMANS 9:33

In nature, gravity, from earth's perspective, pulls things downward, and entropy yanks them apart. The same is true spiritually. We all deal with decline and deterioration—in our bodies, relationships, institutions, and even our aspirations. There is only one place where we will never be disappointed, the place of complete trust in God. Lifestyles, heroes, treasures, and ambitions will ultimately prove to be let-downs, as they are caught in the sweep of "gravity" and "entropy." But God never fails. *Never.*

*But as many as received Him, to them He gave
the right to become children of God, even to those who
believe in His name, who were born, not of blood nor
of the will of the flesh nor of the will of man, but of God.*

JOHN 1:12–13

I 'm afraid I'm jelling into the kind of person I
don't want to be," a fellow told me. There's a big
difference between "jelling" and "forming." Paul
writes his spiritual "children" at Galatia that he
labors so that Christ might be "formed in you"
(Galatians 4:19). God's covenant children are
"predestined to become conformed to the image"
of Christ (Romans 8:29). Apart from Him you
may "jell" into something you don't want to be, but
God's promise is to form you into Christlikeness.

January 9

For I am confident of this very thing,
that He who began a good work in you will perfect
it until the day of Christ Jesus.

PHILIPPIANS 1:6

What God starts, God finishes. That's His promise to you if you are His covenant child through Jesus Christ. But spiritual development is like physical growth, dependent on your cooperation. Stop eating and exercising, and your growth will be stunted. Many people desire a peaceful heart above all. However, we must allow the restless heart to motivate us to one filled with peace. Press into God's promise of completion by allowing Him to develop your whole being through feasting on His Word and "working out" your salvation (Philippians 2:12).

"The thief comes only to steal and kill and destroy;
I came that they may have life, and have it abundantly."

JOHN 10:10

John Piper says we all need to be Hedonists—
pleasure seekers. Strange counsel from a
Christian writer.[1] But Piper is referring to the
pleasure of God's abundant life. God commissioned
Moses to lead His covenant people to the Land of
Promise, the Land of Abundant Living. True
hedonism is leaving the two-bit, low-yield, short-term,
never-satisfying, soul-destroying, God-belittling
pleasures of the world and allowing God to be your
abundance. God promises overflowing spiritual
bounty to those who seek Him above all else.

January 11

*For the one who sows to his own flesh will from
the flesh reap corruption, but the one who sows to the
Spirit will from the Spirit reap eternal life.*

GALATIANS 6:8

How long is forever? Consider the Rock of
Gibraltar, towering 1,400 feet over the
Mediterranean. A sparrow alights on this massive
chunk of limestone and rubs its beak on the
surface. The amount of time it would take that
sparrow to turn Gibraltar to dust would be a
fraction of a second compared to eternity. God's
promise of eternal life is the big focus, not the
whizzing flesh-life. Don't miss the eternal promise
by settling for the short-lived deal.

January 12

*There is now no condemnation
for those who are in Christ Jesus.*

ROMANS 8:1

Barbara Bush, visiting Emperor Hirohito at Tokyo's
Imperial Palace, asked the Japanese prince if his
opulent dwelling was new. "Yes," Hirohito answered.
"Was the old palace so old it was falling down?"
Hirohito replied, "No. You bombed it."[2] Mrs. Bush
could have retorted about the need to restore Pearl
Harbor after the 1941 Japanese attack. The truth is
the only person with the right to condemn another
is the absolutely pure individual. Jesus Christ
alone is qualified to judge humanity. When we
receive Him as Savior, He grants us His absolute
innocence, and we are as pure as our Judge!

"FOR I WILL BE MERCIFUL TO THEIR INIQUITIES, AND I WILL REMEMBER THEIR SINS NO MORE."

HEBREWS 8:12

I'm sure you noticed I left you out of my prayers," said the whiny little boy to his parents as he crawled into bed, offended by their discipline. He was unwilling to let it go. When God forgives us, He no longer lets our sin influence His feelings toward us. He lets it go. The disciples crushed Jesus' heart that night in Gethsemane when they snored while He wept. But Jesus didn't let the failures of His followers influence His future fellowship with them. God's promise of mercy includes the dismissal of every offense we've committed against Him.

*The LORD has done great things for us;
We are glad.*

PSALM 126:3

Some Christians," wrote Charles Spurgeon, "are sadly prone to look on the *dark side* of everything, and to dwell more upon what they have gone through than upon what God has done for them."[3] As you *go through*, don't focus on the growling enemies nor the threatening wilderness, but on the promise. Refuse to let past defeats and pains hobble you. Rather, celebrate what God did in bringing you through the crisis. Remember, He did "great things" for you back there. Keep that fact in the center of your vision as you *go through*, and you will have strength to go on.

For as many as are the promises of God, in Him they
are yes ... God willed to make known what is the
riches of the glory of this mystery among the Gentiles,
which is Christ in you, the hope of glory.

2 CORINTHIANS 1:20; COLOSSIANS 1:27

Winston Churchill said Russia "was a riddle wrapped in a mystery inside an enigma." Old Testament Israel might have felt bundled in mystery. The rabbinic scholars would ponder, predict, and project how the promises of God could all be summed up and made real to humanity. Then, in the New Covenant, the Holy Spirit shows how. Christ is the fullness of the promises, and He indwells those who enter a relationship with Him, bringing the full package of all the promises and their fulfillment!

*For He has satisfied the thirsty soul,
And the hungry soul He has filled with what is good.*

PSALM 107:9

To understand your appetites, think of three concentric circles. The outermost is your "casual appetites," your preferences, ranging from salad dressing to songs. The second circle is your "critical appetites," like vital relationships. The inner circle represents your "core appetites," the deepest hunger and thirst. Dr. Larry Crabb says we try to change our lives and satisfy our needs only on the surface.[4] But we stay hungry and thirsty until we allow God to quench our core thirst and hunger.

The LORD's lovingkindnesses indeed never cease,
For His compassions never fail.
They are new every morning;
Great is Your faithfulness.

LAMENTATIONS 3:22-23

Weary Solomon, depleted and bored, looked at the sunrise and thought, ho-hum, meaningless, same-old-same-old. Jeremiah, who remained faithful to the One above the sun, was prompted by the dawn to shout, "Great is Your faithfulness!" The rising sun reminded the prophet of God's promises—His lovingkindnesses. The Lord was as dependable and constant in His promises to His covenant people as the sunburst over the horizon. Hosea understood, too, and wrote, "As surely as the sun rises, he will appear" (Hosea 6:3 NIV) Let morning light remind you of God's faithfulness to you.

January 18

And we know that God causes all things to work together for good to those who love God, to those who are called according to His purpose.

ROMANS 8:28

A wag said that if he could ask Egypt's ancient Sphinx one question it would be, "Do we live on a friendly planet?" Put that query to a pauper sheltered in a shanty and a billionaire living in a penthouse and, surprisingly, the answer might be the same: "No, it's mean, cruel, happenstance, dog-eat-dog!" Pose the question to a person living in the promise of God's purpose, and even the pauper will tell you the tears and blood are components of joy and victory. God's people know their lives in this world are woven of threads both bright and grim, and they live in the joyful expectancy that the final garment will be lovely and radiant.

*For those whom He foreknew, He also predestined
to become conformed to the image of His Son.*

ROMANS 8:29

Alexander Hamilton, one of America's founders, was born on a Caribbean island, illegitimate and in poverty. In youth, he became a protégé and top aide to George Washington, who shaped him into greatness, sometimes amid the anguish and dangers of the Revolutionary War. The grand purpose toward which God is shaping His covenant child is Christlikeness. We are born outside the Kingdom of God, in spiritual destitution, but God promises to form us into the very image and character of the spotless Son of God. His promise is that everything that happens to His child is aimed at that great purpose.

> "For the LORD your God is a compassionate God;
> He will not fail you nor destroy you nor forget
> the covenant with your fathers which He swore to them.
>
> DEUTERONOMY 4:31

When I was a teenager leaving for a date, my mother always told me, "Edwin, don't forget who you are." Sometimes those of us in covenant relationship with God forget who we are. We behave as if we were in league with the devil rather than Holy God. Yet He never forgets His covenant with us. The promises in His covenant are many and varied, yet God never forgets a single promise He's made to you as His child. We can go forward in confidence when we know—especially in the scary places—that God is there and remembers.

January 21

I can do all things through Him who strengthens me.

PHILIPPIANS 4:13

People in covenant with Jesus Christ lose the word "can't"—in its ultimate sense—from their vocabulary. Paul said, "I can do *all things*" through Christ's strength. What does the assertion of "all things" include? Beatings, stonings, shipwreck, tough journeys, raging rivers, vicious thieves, betrayal by one's own, threats from opponents, urban violence, scary jungles, roaring oceans, scammers, sleepless nights, hunger, thirst, bitter weather.[5] If "all things" referred to boggling miracles or leaping tall buildings, I would have a hard time relating. The promises of Christ's strength have to do with the everyday stuff. That's where we need His strength the most.

"I have come as Light into the world, so that everyone
who believes in Me will not remain in darkness."

JOHN 12:46

The animist believes the world is crammed with
deities who must be appeased. The dark, unseen
world is terrifying. Jesus brings us into relationship
with the Father, and we need no longer shiver
before a myriad of unseen spirits. Knowing God as
Father puts a new light on the seen world as well.
Pain and perspiration and things we don't
understand sometimes mark daily living. But even
that which remains obscure is bathed in the light
of His love. We discover that in His presence,
"even the darkness is not dark" (Psalm 139:12).

January 23

'Do not fear, for I am with you; Do not anxiously look about you, for I am your God. I will strengthen you, surely I will help you, Surely I will uphold you with My righteous right hand.'

ISAIAH 41:10

If you're alone in a frightening forest, you look constantly over your shoulder. No one is protecting your path. But if you're safe in God, He surrounds you like the mountains around Jerusalem (Psalm 125:2). When you know someone is guarding the rear, you can relax, and keep your focus on the path ahead. The good news is that your Father is watching that, too. Your adversary, the devil, prowls like a lion, writes Peter (1 Peter 5:8). But the promise is that God "scrutinize(s) my path and my lying down, and (is) intimately acquainted with all my ways" (Psalm 139:3).

January 24

"When you are cast down,
you will speak with confidence,
And the humble person He will save."

JOB 22:29

The promise echoes throughout the Bible: God resists the proud, but gives grace to the humble (James 4:6; 1 Peter 5:5). Paul defines humility in surprising words: "Be honest in your estimate of yourselves, measuring your value by how much faith God has given you" (Romans 12:3 NLT). I watched a dad teaching his daughter how to ice skate. She was shaky, but knew he wouldn't let go. Her measure of faith in him was based on knowing how much he loved her. She could do little to "help" him skate, and was humbled by the stretch of cold ice. But her assessment of her self-value was in proportion to the confidence she had in the care of her father.

January 25

"The steadfast of mind You will keep in perfect peace,
Because he trusts in You."

ISAIAH 26:3

The steadfast are steady. Ballast is vital in sailing, providing stability in rough seas. Steadfastness of mind is like sturdy strength in a boat's hull. Such balance comes from trust in God. Inner peace is an emotion resulting from a mental action. As you contemplate God's love and faithfulness with your "head," your "heart" responds with peace. Paul writes that as we are stabilized on Christ, "we are no longer to be children, tossed here and there by waves and carried about by every wind of doctrine" (Ephesians 4:14).

January 26

*"Therefore everyone who confesses
Me before men, I will also confess him before
My Father who is in heaven.*

MATTHEW 10:32

What is your outward confession? Eighty-five percent of Americans claim Christianity. But confessing Christianity and confessing Christ may be two different things. Confessing Christ before people means bearing witness to others about Christ and His salvation. That doesn't mean carrying a twenty-pound Bible to work or wearing a six-pound cross around your neck at the mall. Confessing Christ means relating Him to others in the normal flow of your life. If Christ is your Savior and Lord, confessing Him to others is inevitable. And it's just as certain He will confess you before His Father.

January 27

"For as the rain and the snow come down from heaven,
And do not return there without watering the earth
And making it bear and sprout, And furnishing seed to
the sower and bread to the eater; So will My word be
which goes forth from My mouth; It will not return
to Me empty, Without accomplishing what I desire,
And without succeeding in the matter for which I sent it."

ISAIAH 55:10-11

From the micro-world of the soul to the
mega-level of the spiraling galaxies, God's
Word produces its fruit. Fruit is always the match
of its seed. Apple trees don't produce pecans and
pecan trees don't give lemons. Plants yield "after
their kind" (Genesis 1:12). This is why fruit is the
proof of the prophet—and the person (Matthew
12:33). The outcome will show the nature of the
input. God promises that if His Word is embedded
within us, it will produce change in our lives.

January 28

*He heals the brokenhearted and
binds up their wounds.*

PSALM 147:3

If life has hurt you, look inside for healing—
that's the advice the world gives. There are also
counselors who tell you to look outside, at those
who caused you pain. But God gives us better
direction. He knows the broken heart cannot heal
the broken heart. The Father also understands that
focusing on people who hurt us can cause us to fall
into blame and unforgiveness. He calls us to look
up for wellness, not "inside" nor "outside."

January 29

*"For the mountains may be removed
and the hills may shake,
But My lovingkindness will not be removed from you."*

ISAIAH 54:10

There is always more lovingkindness available than there is the stain of sin. Imagine a painting company with the task of putting a fresh coat on every building in America. Initially, there might be concern about where to get that many gallons of paint. But if the Atlantic Ocean were a huge reservoir of paint, the worry would vanish. David, adulterer and murderer, prays, "according to Your lovingkindness . . . blot out my transgressions" (Psalm 51:1). The reservoir of God's grace is inexhaustible. There is always enough for all who repent and ask, and it is never taken away. There is nothing you can do to make God love you more, nor less.

42

January 30

Let the weak say, I am strong.

JOEL 3:10 KJV

Paul thrived on this principle. God told him, "My strength is made perfect in weakness" (2 Corinthians 12:9 KJV), and Paul responded, "When I am weak, then I am strong." This promise was proven in Paul's practical living. Imprisoned in Rome, there were those willing to remind Paul of the nasty things some people had said about him. Then there were the Roman rulers and soldiers who kept him in lock and chain. But rather than being embittered, Paul was "content" (Philippians 4:11). He lived on and by the promises of God, and he knew that though he was a "weak" prisoner, he was strong. History shows he was stronger than Caesar!

January 31

Let us not lose heart in doing good,
for in due time we will reap if we do not grow weary.

GALATIANS 6:9

When I was growing up in Mississippi, my dad had a small country store frequented by farmers. I watched as they came in for fertilizer, seed, hoes, rakes, shovels, and all the other implements of farming. I learned that when the harvest is bad, farmers do three things. First, they look at the soil, then they inspect the seed, and finally, they study the sower. If the soil of your heart is soft and receiving, the seed pure, and the sower faithful, you will see God's harvest in your life. *That's His promise.*

February

February 1

*But if any of you lacks wisdom, let him ask of God,
who gives to all generously and
without reproach, and it will be given to him.*

JAMES 1:5

A thena's statue once towered over the Athens
Acropolis, representing knowledge in the city
of Aristotle, Plato, and other giants of thought in
the ancient capital of philosophy. Athena is still
with us today in the subtle worship of "education,"
the adoration of "knowledge." Knowledge is
quantitative, and wisdom is qualitative. In a highly
technological age, knowledge becomes the goal for
experts building machines that will pack in more
and more data. Without wisdom, knowledge leads
to chaos and disaster. We should never seek
knowledge without first asking God for wisdom to
know how to use the data.

And the ransomed of the LORD will return
And come with joyful shouting to Zion,
With everlasting joy upon their heads.
They will find gladness and joy,
And sorrow and sighing will flee away.

ISAIAH 35:10

Life, liberty, and the pursuit of happiness" were ideals of America's founders. "Happiness," for them, was not wild living, nor endless acquisition, but a content, disciplined, ordered life. The definition has changed. Happiness, as currently understood, can be stolen by circumstances, people, and possessions. Let life situation change, betrayal enter, and possessions be taken, and happiness is yanked. But God's joy is an eternal state of being. His joy can never be stolen.

*Blessed be the God and Father of our Lord Jesus Christ,
who according to His great mercy has caused us to
be born again to a living hope through the resurrection
of Jesus Christ from the dead, to obtain an
inheritance which is imperishable and undefiled and
will not fade away, reserved in heaven for you.*

1 PETER 1:3-4

People are hungry to know what Heaven is like.
A popular TV celebrity conducts mass séances.
Oriental mysticism has us transmigrating from one
body to another until we are merged into the mass of
deity. Muslims believe in seven heavens, full of carnal
pleasures. Heaven was the "happy hunting grounds" for
Native Americans. I believe God intentionally revealed
only a fraction of what Heaven is like. Otherwise,
we'd all be looking for the fastest route there. This
inheritance is not subject to time, entropy, or rust.
God's promise is that we get there on His terms.

February 4

Jesus said to them, "I am the bread of life;
he who comes to Me will not hunger, and he who
believes in Me will never thirst."

JOHN 6:35

Contemporary culture is fascinated by the wolf and celebrates it as a symbol of the full, uninhibited life. In reality, the wolf is a slave to fear, haunted by the night shadows. A better symbol of fullness would be the domesticated dog. The wolfish nature has been tamed. The pet finds a fullness of life denied the wild wolf. The dog with his master enjoys more freedom than the wolf inhabiting the anarchy of the forest. Liberty is found when one is "domesticated" under the Master, Jesus. No longer is such an individual compelled by the basic quest for survival, but he or she lives in the fullness of the Master's supply.

February 5

"I will lead the blind by a way they do not know,
In paths they do not know I will guide them.
I will make darkness into light before them
And rugged places into plains.
These are the things I will do,
And I will not leave them undone."

ISAIAH 42:16

Jimmy Parrish was among my boyhood pastors. He had a son—Jimmy Jr.—who was totally blind. We were the same age, so it became my honor to lead Jimmy Jr. around the church and at school. When I think of God's promise to lead the spiritually blind, I remember my own desire to guide Jimmy Jr. I wanted to steer him away from traps and threats. If I, as a not-so-godly teen wanted to lead Jimmy Jr. with care, how much more God will guide us, who cannot yet see all the wonders of His Kingdom and its truth.

February 6

From Your precepts I get understanding;
Therefore I hate every false way.

PSALM 119:104

In our data-saturated society, we are awash in precepts. We have books, videos, tapes, seminars and Internet streaming. We go to pundits, professors, preachers, psychologists, psychiatrists, and psychotherapists. Everybody layers us with more precepts for healthy living, family-raising, money-making, and tulip-growing. At last we shout, "I don't need any more!" But God's precepts, revealed in His Word, aren't optional. They are not of the "take it or leave it" variety, but vital as the precepts of breathing. For those who take them seriously, God's precepts provide operational reality for living at the highest level.

February 7

"I have seen his ways, but I will heal him;
I will lead him and restore comfort to him
and to his mourners."

ISAIAH 57:18

Old-fashioned medicine shows offered panaceas, tonics that would cure all ills. As good as contemporary medicine is, sometimes all it can offer is a temporary treatment. God, however, promises restoration. The Hebrew word refers to a "covenant of peace." God promises weary human beings transformation, resulting in restoration of exhausted souls. The mind is renewed, the emotions tamed, and the will aligned with that of the Father. This is a cure that lasts.

February 8

> But you are A CHOSEN RACE, A ROYAL
> PRIESTHOOD, A HOLY NATION, A PEOPLE FOR
> God's OWN POSSESSION, so that you may proclaim
> the excellencies of Him who has called you
> out of darkness into His marvelous light.
>
> 1 PETER 2:9

I remember a Bible study group that consisted of doctors, attorneys, CEOs, vice presidents, entrepreneurial geniuses, and a street sweeper. In the initial meeting, the group leader asked each to identify himself. "I am a physician," said one. "I'm an attorney," another responded. "I'm vice president for operations," answered a third. "I am a son of the King," the street sweeper said. He had no identity in the world in which he could boast, but he knew his core identity. The others were clouded by their earthly titles, but the street sweeper knew he was chosen by the King of Kings to be a son.

"If you have faith the size of a mustard seed, you will say to this mountain, 'Move from here to there,' and it will move; and nothing will be impossible to you."

MATTHEW 17:20

Lee Strobel reminds us that in first-century Israel, a great teacher able to solve problems with Scripture was considered an "uprooter" or "pulverizer" of mountains.[6] "Moving" a mountain symbolized getting rid of a difficulty or obstacle. A mustard seed, says Strobel, is 39/1000th of an inch across, but it produces a fast-growing plant that can reach twelve feet in one season. God's promise is that Christ's faith, operating in you and me, is as vital as that mustard plant. It shoves aside doubts, difficulties, obstacles, and barriers to the accomplishment of the will of God in our lives.

February 10

"Again, the kingdom of heaven is like a merchant seeking fine pearls, and upon finding one pearl of great value, he went and sold all that he had and bought it. . . . "But seek first His kingdom and His righteousness, and all these things will be added to you."

MATTHEW 13:45-46; MATTHEW 6:33

Sunrise. Pearl-seeking time. The gem merchant has one passion, one pursuit, one goal for his day: finding the perfect pearl. All other concerns turn to ash in the fire of that objective. Finding the perfect pearl, he doesn't negotiate. He wants it at any price. Sunrises are followed inevitably by sunsets. The sunset is the test of true value. Only the sunset reveals whether the sunrise pursuits were worth it. Jesus promises that if our sunrise quest is God's Kingdom, we arrive at the sunset of life recognizing we have the pearl of great price—and everything else we needed along the way.

55

Therefore if anyone is in Christ, he is a new creature;
the old things passed away; behold, new things have come.

2 CORINTHIANS 5:17

Stephen Hawking, the famous British physicist, said humanity is learning how the universe began.[7] Scientist Robert Jastrow wrote that scholars arriving on that peak of knowledge would find that theologians had been sitting there for centuries.[8] The Bible describes how the world was created and how people are created anew in and by Christ. Genesis says all was in darkness until God spoke light into being. That's the moment of salvation for the individual. Then, Genesis reports, the Holy Spirit "brooded" over the "deep," nurturing life (Genesis 1:2). For the person in Christ, this is growth in Christ's image. God promises that the creative event of the new birth leads to the creative process of becoming a truly new creation in Christ Jesus.

February 12

*For whom the LORD loves He reproves, Even as
a father corrects the son in whom he delights....
"For the Lord disciplines those he loves, and he
punishes those he accepts as his children."*

PROVERBS 3:12; HEBREWS 12:6 NLT

We are to discipline our own children. That's
why the promises of God include His
discipline of us. The Father's discipline is a mark of
the Father's love. A child without discipline may
grow up in anarchy and insecurity, the feeling that
mom or dad didn't care enough to go to the trouble
to provide discipline. Our Heavenly Father loves
us absolutely, and we have the security of knowing
He will set safe boundaries for us in the form of
discipline.

February 13

Who is the man who fears the LORD?
He will instruct him in the way he should choose.

PSALM 25:12

A mother cat, kitten on her back, tried crossing New York City's intersection of 42nd Street and Broadway. Storms of traffic filled the crossroads with chaos. The mother cat repeatedly started across, then retreated after a couple of steps. A policeman suddenly stepped into the maelstrom, and made New York City stand still as the cat and her kitten crossed. The animals had no idea that all the authority of that huge metropolis—symbolized in the officer's badge—had been mobilized on their behalf. God's promise to instruct us in the way we should choose means He mobilizes Heaven's authority and resources to help us in life's wild intersections.

"He who has My commandments and keeps them is the one who loves Me; and he who loves Me will be loved by My Father, and I will love him and will disclose Myself to him."

JOHN 14:21

Love entrusts itself to the beloved. But John 2:24 said He would not entrust Himself to those interested merely in His miracles. God is eager to reveal Himself fully to us, and Jesus is His means of revelation. But curiosity—a matter of the head— won't gain us this level of intimate revelation. Love is an issue of the heart, and Jesus discloses Himself only to those whose hearts are His. Those who seek Him with their heads may know *about* Him, but those who love Him with their hearts will know *Him*.

Bless the LORD, O my soul,
And forget none of His benefits;
Who pardons all your iniquities.

PSALM 103:2-3

Michael Whitman was a British sympathizer during the American Revolution. Peter Miller, a committed Christian, was Whitman's despised neighbor. Whitman was arrested as a traitor and taken to Philadelphia for execution. But Miller trekked through the snow to George Washington at Valley Forge, where he pled for Whitman's life. "I cannot grant you the life of your friend," Washington told Miller. *Friend? Whitman is my worst enemy!*" Washington realized Miller had walked sixty miles to save his adversary and granted the request. We were Christ's enemies, but He treated us as His friends, and laid down His life for us, that we might be pardoned.[9]

February 16

Bless the LORD, O my soul,
And forget none of His benefits;
Who pardons all your iniquities,
Who heals all your diseases.

PSALM 103:2-3

I once made a list of my healings for which I needed to be grateful. "Father, I thank You when I didn't get sick from the zillion germs, viruses, and bacteria to which I have been exposed throughout my life. Thank You for healing me from diseases I did contract, and for creating me with a body designed to throw off sicknesses." All healing is a miracle, whether manifest here or in Heaven, through the direct touch of God or the touch of the Lord through medicine. The promise of God is to heal us, whenever, however, wherever is according to His sovereign plan.

February 17

Who redeems your life from the pit,
Who crowns you with lovingkindness and compassion;
Who satisfies your years with good things.

PSALM 103:4-5

A friend of mine has a ranch. He built a beautiful home there and fenced it off from the acreage where the cattle forage. But the cows ignored the large pastures and finally forced their way into my friend's yard. Once there, however, they became desperate to get out. They found the same brown spots, burrs, and prickly cactus in the yard that grew in the pasture. Similarly, we try to push our way into greener pastures, then, we aren't satisfied, begin looking for a way out. But if you center your quest for satisfaction on God, He will fill you up.

Tebruary 18

Who redeems your life from the pit,
Who crowns you with lovingkindness and compassion;
Who satisfies your years with good things,
So that your youth is renewed like the eagle.

PSALM 103:4–5

It's sad to see an older person become child*ish*, but wonderful to be with a child*like* senior citizen. Eagles go through molting periods so that no matter what their age, they look young and continue to soar with vitality. People in covenant with God are "wow!" focused, not "how?" centered. Some ask, bitterly, "How can this thing happen to me?" But those who let God renew them say, "Wow, I wonder what God is doing in my life through this circumstance!" When you're mature in Christ, even though your bodily strength wanes, your spirit and soul will soar like a young eagle.

"But the one who endures to the end, he will be saved."

MATTHEW 24:13

I was prepared to eat bitterness when I went to China, but not to eat loss," said Mabel Williamson. "Eating bitterness" symbolized suffering and hardship. "Eating loss" meant giving up the right to one's self. Jesus warns that following Him is risky living by worldly standards. Real discipleship means "eating loss," taking up your cross, dying to self. This is the secret to endurance. Mabel Williamson, Hudson Taylor, and many other nameless Old China Hands found the secret, endured to the "end"—which means "purpose"—and saw the promise of God. The Gospel is spreading so fast in China now that it could become the center of global Christianity!

February 20

But we have this treasure in earthen vessels,
so that the surpassing greatness of the power will be of
God and not from ourselves; we are afflicted in
every way, but not crushed; perplexed, but not
despairing; persecuted, but not forsaken;
struck down, but not destroyed; always carrying about
in the body the dying of Jesus, so that the
life of Jesus also may be manifested in our body.

2 CORINTHIANS 4:7-10

God promises we will be broken. Brokenness is essential to our purpose. God assigned Gideon to deliver Israel from the Midianites. The strategy was to place torches in earthen jars, then break the jars on signal. The enemy soldiers turned on one another, thinking they were surrounded. Without brokenness, there was no victory. To the extent we are broken, we manifest the life of Jesus to all those around us.

Therefore, having been justified by faith,
we have peace with God through our Lord Jesus Christ.

ROMANS 5:1

Justification is an event. The moment you trust Christ for forgiveness your status changes in the Court of Eternity from guilty to innocent. Some think justification is a process, but this viewpoint results in a lifelong struggle to earn one's own justification. There is no peace in that struggle, only dread that one may not have done enough to appease the Judge. God promises that when we are justified we have peace with Him, not because of what we do, but because of what He has done.

Jebruary 22

*Therefore, having been justified by faith,
we have peace with God through our Lord Jesus Christ,
through whom also we have obtained our
introduction by faith into this grace in which we stand;
and we exult in hope of the glory of God.*

ROMANS 5:1-2

A man saved to buy a Rolls Royce. The day came when he went excitedly to the dealership. "What's the horsepower on this engine?" he asked. The dealer couldn't find the answer in the brochures, so he emailed the factory in England with the question. "Adequate" was the immediate reply. The car was powerful enough for whatever mountain the driver might confront, whatever desert had to be crossed, whatever load pulled, whatever storm driven through. God's grace is a Rolls Royce. It is adequate for every situation you will face—and then some.

*And not only this, but we also exult in our tribulations,
knowing that tribulation brings about perseverance;
and perseverance, proven character; and proven
character, hope; and hope does not disappoint, because
the love of God has been poured out within our
hearts through the Holy Spirit who was given to us.*

ROMANS 5:3-5

Standing at the base of the Great Pyramid, all I
could see was one side of a triangle. At the
bottom, only a portion of the huge structure was
visible. Flying out of Cairo, I could see the whole.
Tribulation is only one side of our experience. We
must get above and see the whole promise of God,
the complete structure He's creating in our lives.
The Lord will take us to the peak of hope, but that
comes only when our character is tested and
proven through learning to persevere through the
rigors of tribulation.

*"My sheep hear My voice, and I know them,
and they follow Me; and I give eternal life to them, and
they will never perish; and no one will snatch them
out of My hand. My Father, who has given them to Me,
is greater than all; and no one is able to snatch
them out of the Father's hand. I and the Father are one."*

JOHN 10:27-30

Sheep are among the least secure of the world's animals. Turn my dog Sonny loose, and he's wild. Turn a sheep loose, and it just wanders off. Sheep don't swim because of the weight of their wool. They're too afraid to drink from flowing streams. Sometimes they fall over on their backs and can't get up. The only place a sheep is safe is in the hands of its shepherd. We are sheep; Jesus is the Shepherd. He promises us double security because we are in His hand, and He is in the hand of the Father.

February 25

*Yet, with respect to the promise of God, he did
not waver in unbelief but grew strong in faith,
giving glory to God, and being fully assured that what
God had promised, He was able also to perform.*

ROMANS 4:20-21

Claiming God's promises involves what we might call
the "Triple T" maneuver. Abraham demonstrates it.
First is *Trust*. Faith in God means resting all the
weight of your hopes and dreams on Him. *Time* is
second. Abraham trusted God to honor the promise
of a son, but when nothing happened, Abraham
wasn't worried. He knew God has a special moment
for the manifestation of His promises to us, and this
moment is tied to our Kingdom purpose and destiny.
Finally is the *Thrill* of fulfillment of the promise,
when we hold God's promise in our hands and hearts.
Trust in God, submit to His timing, and you'll have
the thrill of manifest promise.

February 26

"But love your enemies, and do good, and lend,
expecting nothing in return; and your reward
will be great, and you will be sons of the Most High;
for He Himself is kind to ungrateful and evil men."

LUKE 6:35

An architect dreams of designing skyscrapers but is assigned to draw mud huts. A composer yearns to write symphonies but is hired only to pen beer-commercial music. Heaven is a world of limitless self-fulfillment. All we do, every gift and talent, will be elevated to a capacity beyond our comprehension. Billy Graham had a friend passing through difficulty. One day he passed a church construction site. "What are you doing?" he asked a stonecutter. "See that little opening up near the steeple? I'm shaping this down here so it will fit up there." God is shaping you "down here" so you will fit "up there."

February 27

For the ways of a man are before the eyes of the LORD,
And He watches all his paths.

PROVERBS 5:21

When our son Ed was four he liked to wander into the woods near our house. I'd retrieve and discipline him, but it did no good. One day I allowed Ed to stray off into the forest. I followed from a distance, hiding behind a tree. Deeper into the woods he went until he finally realized he was lost. Just as he began to cry, I stepped out from my hiding place. "Son, are you ready to go home?" I asked Ed. If you are God's covenant child, He promises to watch your paths. Just when you think it's hopeless, He is there to lead you home.

February 28

*But if any of you lacks wisdom,
let him ask of God, who gives to all generously and
without reproach, and it will be given to him.*

JAMES 1:5

God's wisdom comes through alignment of head and heart. I once hired a person because there was a task many felt he could perform and because I liked him, even though I knew he had personal problems. I prayed for wisdom. My emotions said "Yes," but my mind, "No." I hired him anyway, and he proved to be the wrong person. He was hurt and we suffered. I missed God's wisdom on that matter, because my head and heart were not aligned. God promises us wisdom when we seek it in His way.

*Cast your burden upon the LORD
and He will sustain you;
He will never allow the righteous to be shaken.*

PSALM 55:22

Some jolts are jarring while other jolts are blessed. God will shake you up so that you learn to cast your burden on Him, blessing you with the discovery of how to walk through His sustaining power. Job was jolted severely, yet he came to declare, "Though He slay me, I will hope in Him" (Job 13:15). The jarring jolt led to the blessed jolt, when Job was amazed at how God ultimately blessed him with double that which he had prior to the jarring jolts.

March

For the LORD God is a sun and shield.

PSALM 84:11

If you are God's covenant child through Jesus Christ, nothing can get at you unless it comes through God. I grew up with Saturday matinees at the neighborhood movie theater featuring Gene Autry, Roy Rogers, the Cisco Kid, and other cinema heroes. No matter how much danger they faced, I never worried, because they were protected by the script that guaranteed their safety. Run away from God, and you leave your shield. Walk faithfully under His Lordship, and you can't be taken from the world until He says it's time.

March 2

*About 40,000 equipped for war, crossed for battle
before the LORD to the desert plains of Jericho . . .
"For the eyes of the LORD move to and fro
throughout the earth that He may strongly
support those whose heart is completely His."*

JOSHUA 4:13; 2 CHRONICLES 16:9

Animists believe the world is full of hostile spirits demanding appeasement. Materialists think there is no supernatural dimension, hence no spiritual beings. Biblical Christians know there is a spirit realm and that the supernatural and natural are equally real. However, those trusting Christ walk "before the Lord," confident He is watching over them. While they are aware of their adversary and his aims (1 Peter 5:8), they don't fear the devil and his demons, who watch them to exploit and destroy. If you walk before the Lord, you don't have to fear the other watching eyes.

77

March 3

Who will separate us from the love of Christ?
Will tribulation, or distress, or persecution, or famine,
or nakedness, or peril, or sword?

ROMANS 8:35

God the Absolute loves us absolutely. "Tribulation" can neither squeeze nor thrash us out of His heart. Being hemmed in, cornered, can't remove you from God's love. Pursuit by enemies only drives us deeper into His loving arms. Shameful exposure brings us His compassion. Threatening circumstances result in His passion to protect us. The sword cannot slice us from His unlimited love. The totality of adversity for the child is met with the totality of affection from the Father.

March 4

*But in all these things we overwhelmingly
conquer through Him who loved us.*

ROMANS 8:37

A World War II cartoon portrayed a rifle-bearing
soldier approached by a tank. In one panel, the
GI seemed a tiny, outgunned insect compared to
the metallic monster. But in an adjoining panel,
the artist showed the soldier now armed with a
bazooka. The tank still approaches, but now the GI
is a giant and the tank is toy-sized. When the
resurrection power of Jesus Christ operates in our
lives we are more than adequate for whatever
approaches us. We overwhelmingly conquer through
Him Who empowers us, equips us and enables us.

For I am convinced that neither death, nor life, nor angels, nor principalities, nor things present, nor things to come, nor powers, nor height, nor depth, nor any other created thing, will be able to separate us from the love of God, which is in Christ Jesus our Lord.

ROMANS 8:38-39

A pilot is shot down and lands his fighter jet in the ocean. He is knocked out. The airplane is sinking as a carrier-based helicopter approaches. The rescue team leaps into the sea and slips a harness around the unconscious pilot. He is lifted into the safety of the helicopter. Although he is out cold and cannot hold onto the harness, the harness holds on to him. God's love is so relentless that when we are battered by foes seen and unseen, and have difficulty holding on to Him, He grips us tenaciously.

March 6

No real harm befalls the godly,
but the wicked have their fill of trouble.

PROVERBS 12:21 NLT

What's your worst dread? No fear can match the "real harm" of demonic torment. God promises to spare us that ultimate horror as we walk under His rule. But the promise has a reverse side. Come out from under God's covering, and misery displaces peace and joy. Samson was mighty as long as he was obedient to God. But when he rebelled, there was an accelerating descent into trouble: he slipped, he was knocked down, and finally he was knocked out. Walk under Christ's Lordship and Satan has no authority to harm you.

March 7

"The eternal God is a dwelling place,
And underneath are the everlasting arms;
And He drove out the enemy from before you,
And said, 'Destroy!'"

DEUTERONOMY 33:27

I was a kid trying to balance macho and anxiety the day my dad taught me to swim. Stiff as a pine log, I stepped into the muddy creek. "Relax, son," my dad said. "I'll put my arms under you, and when you begin to sink, I'll be right there." I started sinking, but felt his sturdy arms holding me up. Everything changed knowing his arms were there. I trusted, relaxed, and luxuriated in the security of the arms holding me up. Remember, when you "swim" life's deep holes and muddy waters, your Father's arms are just below the surface.

March 8

I can do all things through Christ
which strengtheneth me.

PHILIPPIANS 4:13 KJV

Paul was an old veteran as he remembered his rugged life. Shipwrecked, stoned, snake bit, beaten, kicked out of towns and cities, left for dead—Paul had experienced it all in his service for Christ. But there was something else he had known, something that transmuted the hard lead of the pain into the pure gold of joy. Paul had learned the richness of the promise of God that he could do and endure anything through Christ's strength. He would never have known that without the agonies he went through. At the end of his earthly life, he concluded that the benefit of God's promise far outweighs the cost (2 Timothy 3:9-11).

Trust in the LORD with all your heart
And do not lean on your own understanding.
In all your ways acknowledge Him,
And He will make your paths straight.

PROVERBS 3:5-6

Christ came to make disciples, not cyborgs. The cyborg, in current science fiction, is a mix of human and mechanical parts, and some people believe God controls them in this type of cold robotic fashion. But God's promise includes both our freedom and His control—a paradox. God lives within us, and we also flow with His life when we are submitted to Him. The person under God's control is the freest of all. A man or woman living through Christ chooses freely, but when they're filled with the Holy Spirit, when they choose what He wants, they automatically choose what they want.

March 10

Do not be wise in your own eyes;
Fear the LORD and turn away from evil.
It will be healing to your body
And refreshment to your bones.

PROVERBS 3:7–8

E very person in covenant with God through
Jesus Christ will be healed, sometimes in this
life, for certain in the eternal. Reverential fear of
the Lord and turning away from evil are two
essentials for healthy living in the here and now.
When you reverence God, you respect what He
has made—beginning with your own body. As you
turn away from evil, you also turn your back on its
byproducts, including unhealthy habits that eat
away at your vitality. For some, the ultimate
description of exhaustion is "bone-weary." God
promises that in Him there is such refreshing it
overcomes tiredness in the extreme.

Honor the LORD from your wealth
And from the first of all your produce;
So your barns will be filled with plenty
And your vats will overflow with new wine.

PROVERBS 3:9-10

God's promise of prosperity is neither a formula nor a magic incantation, but a system. Families, organizations, and whole nations who apply God's principles regarding money enjoy full barns and overflowing vats. Systemic prosperity is "in the package" of the Kingdom of God. "When a man becomes a Christian, he becomes industrious, trustworthy and prosperous," said John Wesley.[10] The more such people there are in a nation, the healthier the economy, the freer the society, and the more prosperous the individual citizens.

March 12

Beloved, now we are children of God,
and it has not appeared as yet what we will be.
We know that when He appears, we will be like Him,
because we will see Him just as He is.

1 JOHN 3:2

A good novelist builds to a climax. The most intriguing fiction is that which hooks us in the beginning with a riddle or a mystery. Writers call this the contract with the reader. The inferred promise is that if the reader will continue to the end, the situation described in the opening lines will be resolved or answered. The lead paragraph of our lives is but the beginning of the story, and God is the Author. The climax is Christ's image manifest in and through us. And, like a good book, the elements mount until it all comes into focus with a satisfying ending.

*God is faithful. He will keep the temptation from
becoming so strong that you can't stand up against it.
When you are tempted, he will show you
a way out so that you will not give in to it.*

1 CORINTHIANS 10:13 NLT

If the person in the adjoining work station dropped
a dollar bill, or perhaps even a fiver, you probably
wouldn't be tempted to keep it. But what if your
ethical threshold were a thousand-dollar bill dropped
within your grasp? God knows your limits. If you
are in covenant with Him, He doesn't interfere
with your freedom, but He curbs the devil's ability
to tempt you to only that which you can handle.
In addition, as His covenant child, you have the
promise of a way out of that tightening passage of
temptation. His power and promise sustain you
when the enticements slither through your life.

"He will wipe away every tear from their eyes;
and there will no longer be any death; there will no
longer be any mourning, or crying, or pain;
the first things have passed away."

REVELATION 21:4

A tear consists of basic elements of life—salt, albumin, and water. Salt preserves and adds flavor, albumin carries protein's strength, and water is life's crucible. When you shed a tear, you're pouring out the whole of life, in miniature. In the span of existence, some people weep themselves dry. You may have experienced heartbreak so intense, you feel there's nothing left inside you. But God wipes the tears and stops the drain of your being. He replenishes the empty vessel from which your tears welled up, and He restores life to its fullness.

March 15

A faithful man will abound with blessings.

PROVERBS 28:20

Integrity leads to abundance. Faithful men and women are trustworthy. I once interviewed two of Houston's most prosperous businessmen. Both are committed to Christ and the advance of His Kingdom through their enterprises. I noted that some people believe one must turn the eye from ethical violations in the workplace. Both these business giants thundered back, "No!" Strong values guided their ascents in the marketplace. They understood the link between integrity and abundance. The two men had applied biblical principles in the commercial world, and they reaped the promise of God.

"Believe in the Lord Jesus, and you will be saved,
you and your household."

ACTS 16:31

S ome think that because their parents believed
in Christ as their Savior that they are
Heaven-bound too. But Acts 16:32 says Paul and
Silas "spoke the word of the Lord to [the Philippian
jailer] together with all who were in his house."
Because the head of the house received Christ,
everyone under his care had opportunity to hear
and respond. God's promise is that when the
pivotal person in a family comes to Christ, it can
lead to the salvation of all in the household.

March 17

For God has not given us a spirit of timidity,
but of power and love and discipline.

2 TIMOTHY 1:7

When the Church is timid, society loses its
prophetic voice. Consider, for example, the
tragedy of a sex-saturated culture. Disease, divorce,
and death run rampant when sexual behavior is
unrestrained. Despite the fact that sex is depicted,
discussed, and deliberated non-stop in popular
media, many churches are silent. God invented
sexuality and meant it to be a blessing. He has
promised His people power, love, and discipline, not
timidity. Jesus' followers shouldn't shy away from
any topic, because the need for truth is vital.

March 18

*"This book of the law shall not depart from
your mouth, but you shall meditate on it day and
night, so that you may be careful to do according to all
that is written in it; for then you will make
your way prosperous, and then you will have success."*

JOSHUA 1:8

The Hebrew words for "prosper" and "success" contain the idea of being wise and insightful. Prosperous and successful people tap into all learning resources possible. Occasionally, someone will ask me if I've read all the books on my personal library shelves. I have to confess I haven't. I own the books, but I don't really possess them because I haven't accessed all their knowledge. This is the way some people pursue Christian living—they don't prioritize learning about God and His ways through Christ. But those who do are "prosperous" and "successful" according to God's promise.

March 19

*Faithful is He who calls you,
and He also will bring it to pass.*

1 THESSALONIANS 5:24

If God calls you to something He's responsible for making it happen. The hammer can build whole houses, but only in the carpenter's hand. The hammer is the instrument, but the carpenter is the builder. God calls us to be tools by which His Kingdom advances in the world. Once we accept the call, it's His business to supply our needs, use us where we fit best, and finish the job. We then work from a position of rest, because He has promised that He is faithful to get the job done through people who are as available to Him as a hammer is to carpenter.

March 20

Train up a child in the way he should go,
Even when he is old he will not depart from it.

PROVERBS 22:6

There are two directions in which a child should go—the *mega* and the *micro*. The mega–direction is toward God and His ways, and the micro is the "bent" of the child. Every parent should be pointing the child to God, and every mom and dad should be observing the child to nurture personality, talents, and gifts. God's promise is that if you lay His truth into the foundation of the child's life, then encourage the development of the child as God has made him or her, you'll produce a solid, consistent, unwavering, fulfilled adult.

March 21

*For the wages of sin is death, but the free gift of God
is eternal life in Christ Jesus our Lord.*

ROMANS 6:23

You have to work for a wage, but God offers a
free gift. Sin is actually labor, but grace is *gratis*—
to you, but not to God. For Ernest Hemingway,
a 1956 interviewer noted, sin seemed to pay off
for life, not death. But sin paid a hefty wage to
Hemingway, even in this life. The final ten years
of his life were spent in emotional and mental
torment. Hemingway killed himself on July 2,
1961. God's promise works both ways—the wages
of sin will always be collected unless one receives
the free gift of Christ's forgiveness.

*For we know that if the earthly tent which is our house
is torn down, we have a building from God,
a house not made with hands, eternal in the heavens.*

2 CORINTHIANS 5:1

Physicians spend their days listening to the woes of sagging tents. Orthopedists deal with the tent pegs, dermatologists the canvas, and the general practitioner the whole structure. Some people—even Christians—fear being tentless, or disembodied after death, because Christ hasn't come yet to clothe them with the resurrection body. However, there is no past, present, or future in eternity; all is the everlasting now. At death the person in Christ leaves the tenses of this dimension, and enters the eternal present-tense. Immediately, he or she is clothed in the resurrection body of Christ, the "building from God."

March 23

As far as the east is from the west,
So far has He removed our transgressions from us . . .
And I will not remember your sins . . .
Yes, You will cast all their sins Into the depths of the sea.

PSALM 103:12; ISAIAH 43:25; MICAH 7:19

When it comes to our sin, there are the "east–west," "amnesia," and "deep sea" promises. Through Jesus Christ, God cleanses us so completely that our guilt is as impossible to find as the dividing line between east and west horizons. God's mercy is so thorough He erases our condemning evil from His mind. God's forgiveness is so sweeping that it's as if our iniquity sinks irretrievably into the deepest ocean trench. Although our accuser seeks something to bring against us, our sin is illusive, non-existent in the mind of Holy God, and cannot be fished out of the depths. God's grace is thorough and complete.

> *"Those who have insight will shine brightly*
> *like the brightness of the expanse of heaven, and those*
> *who lead the many to righteousness,*
> *like the stars forever and ever."*
>
> DANIEL 12:3

I t's easy to take the starry heavens for granted. But walk outside on a cloudless night and the sight can be breathtaking. The brightest object discovered so far in the universe emits about five million-billon times more energy than the sun.[11] With six billion people on earth we seem to live in a universe of humanity. But God promises that the brightest stars are those with insight, who point others in the right direction. Constellations, planets, and individual stars are essential for navigation. The same is true spiritually. People who know God and His ways are able to help others discover direction and destiny.

March 25

*He that goeth forth and weepeth,
bearing precious seed, shall doubtless come again
with rejoicing, bringing his sheaves with him.*

PSALM 126:6 KJV

There is pain and hardship in giving your best when you're uncertain about the harvest. A mother pours her compassion into a child, praying that the soil of the little heart is receptive. A man invests labor and toil in mentoring a lagging associate, wondering if the time and effort are worth it. A teacher struggles to implant truth in a seemingly distracted student. Tears, heartache, sacrifice, and disappointment seem the stuff of sowing. But God's guarantee is that when we sow His Gospel in the fields to which we are assigned, we will see the harvest.

Happy indeed are those whose God is the LORD.

PSALM 144:15 NLT

Relationships are at the core of happiness. An unhealthy codependency, say the psychologists, is one in which a person's happiness is completely dependent upon another's acceptance. For those justified by the grace of Jesus Christ, life's most important relationship is set in order. Jesus reconciles us to the Father. Grace means acceptance that doesn't turn nor fade. To be "accepted in the beloved" (Ephesians 1:6 KJV) is to be in eternal relationship with the One Who matters most. Happy indeed are those whose God is the Lord!

March 27

I know that everything God does will remain forever;
there is nothing to add to it and
there is nothing to take from it, for God has
so worked that men should fear Him.

ECCLESIASTES 3:14

Albert Speer, Hitler's architect, wrote of the Nazi tyrant's passion for monumental buildings that would exalt himself. Speer said Hitler wanted structures built by the theory of "ruin value." He ordered Speer to consider what the monuments would look like in a thousand years, and design them to maintain their grandeur. There is no "ruin value" to be considered in God's works. What He does in a human life is "renewed day by day" (2 Corinthians 4:16). Rather than deterioration, there is development until the Great Day of the Lord, when all in Him reaches its telos—purpose and completeness to which nothing can be added.

"Behold, I stand at the door and knock; if anyone hears My voice and opens the door, I will come in to him and will dine with him, and he with Me."

REVELATION 3:20

Jesus won't climb into your life by a back window. He stands at the door and knocks. When the devil seeks to control you he probes for the weak places he can exploit. When Jesus seeks entry into your heart to bring His marvelous transformation, He gives you the freedom to open the door—or leave it shut. In the ancient Middle East, supper was the best meal of the day. It was when people sat back and celebrated work done and the promise of the new day. Jesus knocks at your heart's door to sup with you. Let in Satan and he snatches everything on the table. Allow Jesus into your life, and He brings the feast with Him.

March 29

"He who overcomes, I will grant to him to sit down with Me on My throne, as I also overcame and sat down with My Father on His throne."

REVELATION 3:21

Old iron bedstead religion" is firm on each end, but sags in the middle. On one end, a person receives Christ as Savior, and is exuberant at the launch of his walk in the Lord. On the other end, someone is approaching earthly life's end, confident and firm in the assurance of Heaven. But between the exuberance of the New Birth and the quiet assurance of eternal security, there's a middle stage in the Christian life. The overcomers are those who experience victory in the middle, when the initial exuberance is years in the past and the final lap decades into the future. Overcomers are firm in the middle.

March 30

*For the eyes of the Lord are over the righteous,
and his ears are open unto their prayers: but the face
of the Lord is against them that do evil.*

1 PETER 3:12 KJV

Who can pray? God listens only to the righteous. A person can communicate only within a realm where he or she exists. The righteous are those whose life is in Christ. To receive Christ's life as one's own makes a person alive in the Kingdom of God, where he and she are able to communicate with God. Until then, there is only one prayer He hears: "Lord, I believe. Save me." This prayer, offered by a person outside Christ, is kicking at the womb, signaling the desire to be born. Once God hears that initial prayer, He also hears all others of the person who is born in Christ and robed in His righteousness.

March 31

*Humble yourselves in the presence of the Lord,
and He will exalt you.*

JAMES 4:10

From the world's perspective, Christ brings the upside-down Kingdom. His realm is one in which the meek conquer, the child gets what the scholar misses, the foolish confound the wise, and the humble rise up. The crippled man at Pool Bethesda waited thirty-eight years for a lift into the water. Jesus told him to forget the water; just do what He asked, and the man would rise up (John 5:8). The world's way is to find the crutches that will hold us up until we get to the waters of success. In the upside-down Kingdom, we humble ourselves before the Master and find ourselves exalted.

April

April 1

Every prudent man acts with knowledge,
But a fool displays folly.

PROVERBS 13:16

My dad loved April Fools' Day because he was
a practical jokester—the rare breed who
enjoyed others pulling shenanigans at his expense.
It's fun to be foolish one day a year, but it's tragic
when such becomes a lifestyle. God promises that
the "prudent"—the shrewd and sensible people—
act with perceptive skill or savvy. The fool, on the
other hand, is the individual who barrels through
life with thoughtless stupidity. You may be a
fun-loving practical joker today, but be sure to
resume your prudent walk tomorrow.

April 2

*A good man leaves an inheritance
to his children's children, and the wealth of the
sinner is stored up for the righteous.*

PROVERBS 13:22

The Kingdom of God is the consuming focus of all God's promises to His people. "Thy Kingdom come," prayed Jesus in His opening statement of the Model Prayer (Matthew 6:10). "Seek first His Kingdom and His righteousness, and all these things will be added to you," Jesus taught His disciples (Matthew 6:33). The "wealth of the sinner" isn't for the enrichment of the righteous individual, but for the advancement of the Kingdom, which is the mission of people made righteous in Christ. God promises that from the world itself will come financial and material resources for the spread of the Kingdom that will transform the world.

"In My Father's house are many dwelling places;
if it were not so, I would have told you; for I go to prepare
a place for you. If I go and prepare a place for you,
I will come again and receive you to Myself,
that where I am, there you may be also."

JOHN 14:2–3

Jo Beth and I flew from Amsterdam to New York. Seated near us was a three-generational family of excited Russian emigrants. They were headed for California, where a son had already moved and established a home. I couldn't help but think of the tears when that boy announced he was leaving Russia. But then I began to imagine the homecoming. Knowing the vast differences between Russia and California, I was certain the new home would be better than their minds could grasp. *The* Son has your place ready in your true home—and it's more fabulous than you can imagine.

"*Behold, I have given you authority to tread on serpents and scorpions, and over all the power of the enemy, and nothing will injure you*" ... *And the Lord said to Paul in the night by a vision, "Do not be afraid any longer, but go on speaking and do not be silent; for I am with you, and no man will attack you in order to harm you, for I have many people in this city."*

LUKE 10:19; ACTS 18:9–10

Jesus promised His followers that as long as we are under Him, we have His authority, including power over the "serpents" and "scorpions," symbolizing demons. So Paul was bullet-proof when he headed for Corinth. When you're in the center of God's will, you need not be afraid. So, under Christ's Lordship, you have the authority, not the devil. The adversary can't take you out of the world. Only God can do that, and He won't until your mission is completed.

April 5

Submit therefore to God.
Resist the devil and he will flee from you.

JAMES 4:7

Submitting and resisting are the actions for
overcoming the entrapments, snares, wiles,
and schemes of the devil. "Submit," here, is a
military word. A private recognizes who's in charge,
and it's not him, but the general. Resistance is
modeled by Jesus in His temptations. He counters
every satanic lie with the truth of God's Word.
God's promise is that the devil will scamper away
from you as quickly as possible when he sees Christ
over you and collides with God's truth within you.

April 6

For He has satisfied the thirsty soul,
And the hungry soul He has filled with what is good.

PSALM 107:9

No thirst, no satisfaction; no hunger, no fullness. Thirst proves the existence of water, and hunger the reality of food, for if water and bread did not exist, we would not desire them. The need for God evident in humanity from the beginning of time is proof of God's existence. A whole branch of science has emerged, studying the way the brain is "hardwired for God."[12] Our need for God is real, and so is He, otherwise we would not yearn for Him. And those who seek Him will be satisfied.

April 7

"For the LORD GOD is my strength and song,
And He has become my salvation."
Therefore you will joyously draw water
From the springs of salvation.

ISAIAH 12:2-3

Trying to slake its thirst, humanity has drunk from many wells in its trek through history. Cain gulped deep from the fountain of power, and remained dry. His descendants at Babel sought satisfaction with technological achievement, but stayed thirsty. Zipping forward in time, medieval thinkers dipped into the trough of philosophy, Enlightenment scholastics sipped rationalism, modern man slurped from science, and post-modern humanity drank from the occult. Yet thirst is pandemic. God alone is the well in the desert of existence, and those who go to Him to satisfy their parched souls find an inexhaustible fount.

April 8

*"I am the living bread that came down
out of heaven; if anyone eats of this bread,
he will live forever; and the bread also which I will
give for the life of the world is My flesh."*

JOHN 6:51

Manna sustained the Jews in the wilderness, but Jesus, the "living bread," came to bring more than mere survival. Existing is quantitative, measured in time, but living is qualitative, stretching through eternity and encompassing time. Yet the ancient manna foreshadowed Jesus in a sense. The word *manna* means, "What is it?" Jesus was a mystery to those who saw Him. The manna fell at night, so Jesus came into the world's darkness. Manna was God's gift to the people; all they had to do was receive it. So with Jesus. He is God's gift, and even better than manna, He provides life, not measly existence.

April 9

And do not get drunk with wine,
for that is dissipation, but be filled with the Spirit.

EPHESIANS 5:18

Wynn, a corn chip fanatic, received a call from a friend for whom he had done a favor. "Tomorrow night I'm buying you the biggest steak in town!" Wynn fasted all the next day. But an hour before dinner, his buddy phoned. "My car is busted, and I can't make it." Desperate, Wynn swallowed a bag of corn chips, washing it down with a can of pop. Just then his pal called. "Car's running after all." But Wynn was so full of corn chips and pop he had no room for steak. Don't fill up your life with junk and miss the promise of the Holy Spirit's fullness.

For thus says the high and exalted One
Who lives forever, whose name is Holy,
"I dwell on a high and holy place,
And also with the contrite and lowly of spirit
In order to revive the spirit of the lowly
And to revive the heart of the contrite."

ISAIAH 57:15

God is omnipresent, yet has locality or "thereness." He occupies the Throne of the cosmos, positioned at its summit. Yet in His creation, God chooses to localize His presence with the lowliest of people. Our city, Houston, is prone to flooding. Torrential rains fall from the high place of the skies and flow relentlessly along the ground until they run into the lowest places. It is a picture of God. He is transcendent, yet immanent, high and lifted up, yet near. And He comes to those who need Him.

*Surely goodness and lovingkindness will
follow me all the days of my life,
And I will dwell in the house of the LORD forever.*

PSALM 23:6

God's promise for those in covenant with Him is that they will be stalked people. Goodness and lovingkindness will follow them throughout life. God chases His people with "goodness," that which is for their benefit and wellbeing. His lovingkindness is His unfailing love and favor. This, too, tracks us. We need to look over our shoulders and make sure we're not trying to outrun the blessing that pursues us.

April 12

And the work of righteousness will be peace,
And the service of righteousness,
quietness and confidence forever.

ISAIAH 32:17

Y ou can't buy a truly good sleep; it's God's gift. You can take pills and potions to knock you out, but that's not a good sleep. The best of sleeps comes after you've worked hard, accomplished a mission, relished the success, and then plunged into a warm bed. Many people labor all day and toss all night. Perhaps it's because they're not in the service of righteousness. Peace, quietness, and confidence result when you've given the best of yourself to the best of tasks.

April 13

For thus the Lord GOD, the Holy One of Israel, has said,
"In repentance and rest you will be saved,
In quietness and trust is your strength."

ISAIAH 30:15

Somebody got my goat!" People say that
sometimes when rankled and upset. The phrase
came from horseracing. Trainers trying to calm a
high-strung horse on the night before a race
would put a goat in the stall with the horse. The
presence of the calm goat would quiet the horse.
Occasionally, an opponent would steal the goat
prior to the race, hence the saying. When we turn
from the sin, guilt, and worries that make us tense
and tight, we rest. As the lifestyle of trust in God
develops in our souls, we find our strength and are
settled in His quietness.

"He who has My commandments and
keeps them is the one who loves Me; and he who loves
Me will be loved by My Father, and I will love him
and will disclose Myself to him."

JOHN 14:21

Our media-saturated, litigation-oriented society applauds "full disclosure," but it sneers at "spin," which is the effort to contort facts so they seem not to be what they are. Jesus desires to disclose Himself fully to His people, no spin, no facts concealed, no fine print. He won't entrust Himself to the masses, because He understands human nature (John 2:25). But those in intimate "blood" relation to Him through His salvation covenant will know Him fully. Throughout a life devoted to Christ, His mind will gradually expand in the soul of His beloved, transforming the worldview of each of His disciples.

April 15

I will counsel you with My eye upon you.

PSALM 32:8

The devil watches you to steal, kill, and destroy (John 10:10), and his demons observe you to exploit your flaws. But God watches you to counsel you. The Hebrew term for *counsel* means "to consult together." When you seek the advice of another human, you must describe situations and circumstances. But God's counsel is like that of a father watching his child learn to drive. The dad doesn't instruct from a distance with his cell phone; rather, he's there in the front seat. "Steer to the left," he says; "put on the brakes a little," he instructs. Similarly, God is in the front seat with you, gently guiding you through every turn.

Light arises in the darkness for the upright.

PSALM 112:4

L ight be!" was God's first creative command (Genesis 1:3). In that instance, the switch was flipped, and the darkness displaced. Since that moment, the darkness has never been able to overwhelm the light (John 1:5). The "upright"— those depending on Christ's goodness as their own—will journey through dark passages, seasons of trial and tribulation. But they will discover that down in the gloom of the deep, God will speak once more His "Light be!" and their night will be bright as day (Psalm 139:12).

April 17

Commit your works to the LORD
And your plans will be established.

PROVERBS 16:3

I believe very profoundly in an over-ruling Providence, and I do not fear that any real plans can be thrown off the track," said Woodrow Wilson.[13] Works that can be submitted to God have plans that will succeed, even if the planners get some details wrong. God sees the final outcome of all things. He allows us the privilege of being "co-laborers" with Him. However, like a master observing an apprentice, He steps in when our plans aren't aligned with the big picture, and He puts them right.

April 18

*But we have this treasure in earthen vessels, so that the
surpassing greatness of the power will be of God and
not from ourselves; we are afflicted in every way, but not
crushed; perplexed, but not despairing; persecuted, but
not forsaken; struck down, but not destroyed; always
carrying about in the body the dying of Jesus, so that the
life of Jesus also may be manifested in our body.*

2 CORINTHIANS 4:7–10

The piñata is the delight of any party. Small kids
to senior adults can be seen blindfolded, thrashing
away to shatter the dangling shape. They know
that the more the piñata is broken, the faster its
treasures will spill out, and in greater quantity.
God's purpose and promise for His covenant people
is that they allow the treasure of Jesus' life to pour
out from them upon others. But Christians are like
piñatas: they must be broken before the delights
inside them can be enjoyed by other people.

April 19

The one who guards his mouth preserves his life;
The one who opens wide his lips comes to ruin.

PROVERBS 13:3

The big danger in swallowing your foot is that you may choke on it as it goes down. Guards are stationed at boundaries. "Free speech" does not mean liberty to blurt out one's limited knowledge, mistaken conclusions, unproven assumptions, and acidic gossip. Such foolishness leads to ruin. God promises protection to those who establish the boundaries of His truth and wisdom around their mouths. Specifically, God's pledge is that His people maintain the wellness of their souls, not just their bodies. When you're tempted to shoot off your mouth, prayer will help you keep the safety on instead.

April 20

*The effective prayer of a righteous man
can accomplish much.*

JAMES 5:16

Godly Daniel prays and it seems forever before there's an answer. At last an angel stands before him and recounts the struggle of battling his way from Heaven through the principalities and powers of the air—a fight so fierce that mighty Michael, an archangel, had to reinforce him (Daniel 10:10–14). This is not the state of prayer today. Jesus plowed a hole right through the dominion of the demonic, and every time we pray, our prayers follow his trail right to the Throne of God.

April 21

*But I say, walk by the Spirit, and you
will not carry out the desire of the flesh.*

GALATIANS 5:16

T he Holy Spirit is telling me to divorce my wife,"
the man said to his pastor. Despite the minister's
counsel otherwise, the husband brought misery to
his family as he left his spouse. The Holy Spirit
doesn't contradict the Holy Spirit. Acting—
walking—by the Spirit doesn't mean moving upon
every emotional impulse. Rather, it's like a man
pulled over by a policeman. The officer wants to
check the driver's sobriety, and lays a straight tape
on the ground. "Walk by that line!" the patrolman
says. Walking "by" the Spirit is behaving according
to His ways, no matter what your emotions or
imaginations may be telling you to do.

Finally, brethren, whatever is true, whatever is honorable, whatever is right, whatever is pure, whatever is lovely, whatever is of good repute, if there is any excellence and if anything worthy of praise, dwell on these things. The things you have learned and received and heard and seen in me, practice these things, and the God of peace will be with you.

PHILIPPIANS 4:8-9

D welling on *truth* brings you peace, because you know your foundation will never crack. Residing on the *honorable* is peaceable, because there are no skeletons in the closet. Dwelling on that which is *right* brings the peace of knowing the timbers are straight and the structure level. Living on the *pure* is peaceful, because there're no corruptive bugs to eat away the foundations. The God of peace will be with you, because you're living where He lives.

April 23

*Therefore, prepare your minds for action, keep sober
in spirit, fix your hope completely on the grace
to be brought to you at the revelation of Jesus Christ.*

1 PETER 1:13

To the occultist, an encounter with a supernatural
being can hold dread. Has the creature been
properly appeased? Those in Christ don't have
anxiety about their ultimate meeting with Him.
Since receiving Christ as Savior, they have armored
their minds with the promise of His grace and
moved through life's challenges with His favor at
the center of their thoughts. They lean into His
coming again at the peak of history, when every
eye will see Him, anticipating the full manifestation
of His grace in their lives. Some will scream
despairingly, "Oh, no, *Jesus Christ* is Lord!" But
grace-girded folk will exclaim, "Hallelujah, Jesus
Christ *is* Lord!"

April 24

The wicked is thrust down by his wrongdoing,
But the righteous has a refuge when he dies.

PROVERBS 14:32

Some see death as termination, but those trusting Christ view it as transit. At death, the body heads for the ground, but where does the soul go? For those without Christ's eternal life, there is the anxiety of disembodiment, thrust into the dark abyss as a homeless, roofless, wall-less entity. But in Christ, there is the promise of the new body, the new city, the new community, and the new creation wherein is refuge and safety forever. No wonder Saint Teresa reportedly said as she was dying, "Welcome, sister death!" It's the passage by which one enters Christ's refuge.

April 25

*For you have died and your life is
hidden with Christ in God.*

COLOSSIANS 3:3

Hide-and-seek is a fun game for children, but it's shockingly real. The devil constantly searches for someone to rob, kill, destroy and devour (John 10:10; 1 Peter 5:8). Like the kid who is "It," the destroyer and his demons shake every bush and look behind every tree for prey. But whatever is in Christ doesn't even exist in the place where Satan searches. The individual whose life resides in Jesus Christ is concealed in Him. The demons tremble in His presence; therefore all you place in Christ is impregnable.

April 26

A joyful heart is good medicine,
But a broken spirit dries up the bones.

PROVERBS 17:22

Down in the core of the engine room of the nuclear submarine *Thresher*, a leak developed in corroded pipes. The deadly dribble, it's thought, became a spew, fouling the electrical system, and sending the sub down in 8,400 feet of water with all hands. Similarly, what happens in your core—your heart—is vital for your whole being. You sink or swim based on your heart-condition. Joy is the fruit of the Holy Spirit (Galatians 5:22). When that joy spreads, it even heals your "corroded pipes."

*He Himself has said, "I WILL NEVER DESERT YOU,
NOR WILL I EVER FORSAKE YOU."*

HEBREWS 13:5

A mong people's greatest fears is that of abandonment. It's engrained in us since we lost the fellowship of the Father in Eden. We focus on our own dread of abandonment, but God's Spirit is grieved by our absence. Jesus Christ comes to get us back, to restore us to the Father's heart. Like a parent recovering a kidnapped child, once we're back in His arms, He promises never to let us go. Moreover, the mom or dad of the restored child is resolute in the determination never to be away from that little one again. Once safe in Christ, no power seen or unseen can remove Him from you.

*Therefore I am well content with weaknesses,
with insults, with distresses, with persecutions, with
difficulties, for Christ's sake; for when I am weak,
then I am strong.*

2 CORINTHIANS 12:10

Paul could operate in his own strength or God's.
For the power of the Lord to work through Paul,
his own had to be diminished. The man who headed
for Damascus, "breathing threats and murder
against the disciples of the Lord" (Acts 9:1), was a
hard-headed, strong-willed character, arrogant in
his own might. Such a person is unusable as an
instrument of Christ's Kingdom because God "resists
the proud" (James 4:6; 1 Peter 5:5). Thus the
equation of strength, Paul discovered, included the
"W-Factor." To the extent his flesh was weakened,
God's power could take over.

*A righteous man who walks in his integrity—
How blessed are his sons after him.*

PROVERBS 20:7

Integrity leaves a stream of blessing in its wake. The greatest gift you can give your child is a godly life. "I'm not inclined to be religious," someone says. "I'm not very pious," a man echoes. "I'm not oriented to the Bible," a woman declares. All this is like saying, "I don't use electricity because I'm not scientifically bent." Godly living is not about religion, but life. "Righteousness" is a lifestyle conforming to God's holy character. "Integrity"— a consistent and unimpeachable life—flows from it. All who swim in the wake are enriched.

April 30

"Though He slay me,
I will hope in Him.
Nevertheless I will argue my ways before Him.
This also will be my salvation,
For a godless man may not come before His presence.

JOB 13:15–16

There was a remarkable lack of self–interest in Job's love for God. He loved the Lord for His own sake, and not for the blessings God gave. This is a mark of maturing faith. Many of us begin our walk with God because we desire His good gifts. He loves us and receives us where we are. But spiritual growth means continuing to love Him when the gifts seem chunks of coal in a brown bag. Then we experience one of the greatest of His blessings—knowing that God loves us, and, in the end, will resolve life's mysteries and miseries.

May

May 1

*"Ask, and it will be given to you; seek, and you will
find; knock, and it will be opened to you.
For everyone who asks receives, and he who seeks finds,
and to him who knocks it will be opened."*

MATTHEW 7:7-8

Jesus' followers walk in expectancy. Jesus has
given His people the key to the chest of treasures
of God's promises. *Ask, seek, knock* are its three
prongs. He authorizes us to expect a response
lining up with God's perfect will for us. A simple
request becomes earnest seeking that becomes
passionate knocking. People in Christ's covenant,
therefore, walk in the glorious expectancy that
behind the door is the promise that is precise to
fulfill the need.

May 2

He who walks righteously and speaks with sincerity,
He who rejects unjust gain . . .
And shuts his eyes from looking upon evil;
He will dwell on the heights, . . .
His water will be sure.
Your eyes will see the King in His beauty;
They will behold a far-distant land.

ISAIAH 33:15-17

World-weariness is a disease of our age. We are wearing ourselves out in the attempt to gain success, be entertained, and stay ahead. World-weariness spreads as we grapple with scammers seeking unjust gain, entertain ourselves with violence, and spend hours gazing at big-screen evil. At the end of the day such things wear us out. But the person who rejects the exhausting contemporary cultural pit and concentrates on the beauty of the Lord dwells exuberantly on the heights.

May 3

It is God who is at work in you,
both to will and to work for His good pleasure.

PHILIPPIANS 2:13

The Holy Spirit told Paul and Barnabas to move out, but He didn't provide an itinerary. They chose to go to Cyprus because it was a logical place to start. It was Barnabas's hometown, some of the people who launched the Antioch church were there, providing a base of contacts. They went with confidence God was in their choice. They lived the Proverbs 3:5–6 principle, trusting Him with all their heart, leaning not on their own understanding, and acknowledging Him in all their ways. Then they made the most natural choice, only to discover it was the supernatural direction.

May 4

Yet those who wait for the LORD
Will gain new strength;
They will mount up with wings like eagles,
They will run and not get tired,
They will walk and not become weary.

ISAIAH 40:31

Sometimes we experience soaring, excitement, and humdrum—all in one day! We're up there with the eagles, then running with the sprinters, but later we fade to a wearied lope. What happens to the body need not occur in the soul, but what happens in the soul can energize the body. To "wait for the Lord" is to be assured that His wings are under us before we leap into the sky. To "run and not get tired" is to dash into the day with the anticipation of God's faithfulness for all our challenges. If we wait on Him, soar on Him, run in Him, we will walk home at the end of the day energized for the next.

May 5

*"Whatever you ask in My name, that will I do,
so that the Father may be glorified in the Son.
If you ask Me anything in My name, I will do it."*

JOHN 14:13-14

God is omniscient, but He doesn't respond to mere wishes. We must ask because it's an act of our freewill. Further, we must ask in the name of Jesus. Prayer is a covenant matter: only those in Christ have the authority to ask. Our earthly mission is advancing His Kingdom. Therefore, asking in His name, by default, is requesting that which will enable us to carry out our mission. Asking for personal indulgences not related to the Kingdom mission is not asking in Jesus' name, because He is synonymous with the Kingdom. But whatever we ask in alignment with Jesus, His Kingdom and our mission in it, we receive.

May 6

The LORD is my shepherd, I shall not want.

PSALM 23:1

This is easy!" I thought when I first became a Christian. Trust Jesus, He takes away the penalty of our sin, and that's it. Then a Sunday school teacher explained Christian behavior. "This is hard," I concluded. I discovered concepts like unlimited forgiveness, turning the other cheek, and going the second mile. "This is impossible!" I thought. So I passed through the "easy," "hard," and "impossible" stages of Christian growth and arrived at a fourth—emptiness. That's the point at which the Good Shepherd can fill us up. We have to come to the empty stage before we "want," and we have to "want" before we can be filled.

May 7

He makes me lie down in green pastures;
He leads me beside quiet waters.

PSALM 23:2

When I was little I begged dad to let me mow
and hoe, but he said I was too small. Then I
grew. I mowed, and decided hoeing was better.
After hoeing, bagging groceries at our country store
seemed preferable. Finally I reached a disappointing
conclusion—*there ain't no green grass!* God's green
pastures span the heart yielded to Him. Paul said
he was content *anywhere* (Philippians 4:11). If you're
looking for green pastures in circumstances and
places, you'll find them browning over when you
get there. Let God lead you to the green pastures of
the heart, and you will find lushness no matter
where you are.

May 8

He restores my soul;
He guides me in the paths of righteousness
For His name's sake.

PSALM 23:3

When Tolstoy tired, he would plow barefooted, and the feel of dirt on his feet was therapeutic. In nature, there's a link between earthy things such as green pastures, still waters, and a restored soul. The natural mirrors spiritual truth. God's green pastures silence the cacophony of Babylon. His still waters out sparkle the world's muddy gutter streams. In Him, the mind is freed to roam the broad pastures of His truth, the emotions soothed by the rippleless waters, and the will refocused on His paths of righteousness. Nature beckons us to God, not to itself.

*Even though I walk through
the valley of the shadow of death,
I fear no evil, for You are with me;
Your rod and Your staff, they comfort me.*

PSALM 23:4

I have attended university graduation ceremonies
that included honoring a distinguished former
student. When the person's named was called, a
prominent member of the board or administration
would escort the honoree to the stage. If you are in
covenant with God through Jesus Christ, when
your name is sounded at your eternal graduation,
the Son of God Himself will escort you across the
zone between the material and spiritual worlds. He
not only promised to go and prepare a place for us,
but to come again and escort us home.

May 10

You prepare a table before me in the presence of my enemies;
You have anointed my head with oil;
My cup overflows.

PSALM 23:5

The shepherd searched for a tableland for his
sheep. Craggy slopes wouldn't do, because the
animals could fall. When he found the flat stretch,
the shepherd cleared it of threats to the sheep. He
located a water source, and then hacked out a
sheepfold. Though the enemy—lions and bears—
looked hungrily into the perimeter, the sheep
rested in the sheepfold, on the tableland prepared
by the shepherd. If Christ is your shepherd, His
broad arms are the sheepfold, which is planted on
the rich tableland of the Father's care.

May 11

Surely goodness and lovingkindness will
follow me all the days of my life,
And I will dwell in the house of the LORD forever.

PSALM 23:6

Where do you live?" the young initiate into a secret Nazi order was asked. "Stuttgart," he replied. "Wrong!" "Germany!" "Wrong!" "Sir I don't know the answer," the bewildered youth said. "Tell people you live in Hitler!" the officer said. But as a war prisoner in England, the German became a Christian. "I live in Christ," he told people. If God is the world in which you live now, when death comes, you continue to live in eternity where you dwelt in the earth. And while here, if you live in God, no matter where you go, you never leave your dwelling place.

May 12

*But God demonstrates His own love toward us,
in that while we were yet sinners, Christ died for us.*

ROMANS 5:8

When we were at our worst, God gave us His best. All forms of human love have some measure of self interest attached. The Greek New Testament language provides us understanding of the nuances of love. *Eros*-love brings the mutual satisfaction of physical love. *Phileo*-love enables people to share friendship affections. To describe God's love, the Holy Spirit inspired the human Bible writers to use a term rarely employed by the Greeks—*agape*, unconditional love. Nothing displays this word like Jesus dying for us on the cross while we were still in rebellion.

*My little children, I am writing these things to you
so that you may not sin. And if anyone sins, we have an
Advocate with the Father, Jesus Christ the righteous.*

1 JOHN 2:1

You have died and are standing before God. "Let
me tell you about Bill," Satan snarls. The accuser
reads a long list of your sins. "This document tells
of Bill's violations of My Law, right?" God the
Father asks. "I'd like to say a word about Bill," God
the Son says. "He received Me as his Savior and
Lord, repented of his sins, and every accusation
Satan has brought against him is removed by My
blood." With that, the Father—the Judge—yanks
the list of accusations from Satan's hand, tears it
up, and throws it away (Colossians 2:14). If you're
in Christ, you have an Advocate whose testimony
is final.

May 14

*"These signs will accompany those who have believed:
in My name they will cast out demons, they will speak
with new tongues; they will pick up serpents, and if
they drink any deadly poison, it will not hurt them;
they will lay hands on the sick, and they will recover."*

MARK 16:17-18

In war, infantry will slog their way to a head-on encounter with the enemy, and they must have the resources appropriate to the moment. A field commander radios map coordinates to a fighter squadron, circling overhead. Suddenly a barrage from the sky strikes the foe. God's promise to His people on Kingdom mission is to provide what they need, when they need it, and on the right coordinates. The Church loses the big point when it gets sidetracked debating the resources God gives. Instead, she is to go forward on the promise of His supply for what we need in each situation.

May 15

He who walks with integrity, and works righteousness,
And speaks truth in his heart.
He does not slander with his tongue,
Nor does evil to his neighbor,
But who honors those who fear the LORD;
He who does these things will never be shaken.

PSALM 15:2-5

Straight living leads to steady living. Jack had lived a shady, shaky life. Then he met Christ and became a serious follower. The best thing about his new life was that he was no longer afraid, he told me. "What were you afraid of?" I asked. Jack told how he feared the husbands of women with whom he'd had illicit relationships, along with the fear of discovery. His lifestyle was the envy of partiers, but it shrouded him in fear. The purity and integrity of living in Christ's way meant that Jack could no longer be shaken by his old anxieties.

154

May 16

The Son of God appeared for this purpose,
to destroy the works of the devil.

1 JOHN 3:8

A friend of mine waited after a banquet for a parking attendant to bring his car. A woman's auto came first, and she got in as the motor idled. Suddenly her accelerator jammed, and the car sped out of control toward people leaving a restaurant. Thankfully, no one was injured. Had the woman turned off the ignition, the danger would have ended immediately. When Jesus destroyed the works of the devil at the cross, the Greek term for "destroy" means He made Satan's power inoperable. If you are God's covenant child through Christ, you don't have to race through life under the devil's control.

May 17

No one who is born of God practices sin,
because His seed abides in him; and he cannot sin,
because he is born of God.

1 JOHN 3:9

Here is a scary promise: No one born of God practices sin. The Greek tense refers to continual action, and the verse is saying that people who continue a lifestyle of sin don't have God's "seed" in them. But the meaning goes deeper, because not even pagans sin every moment. Many Christians practice sin management rather than genuine growth in Christ. As followers of Christ, our testimony should be, "I'm not perfect yet, but that's my goal!" Focusing on the goal and following spiritual disciplines is positive, dynamic forward movement, rather than the stodgy, stultifying labor of mere sin management.

May 18

*His divine power has granted to us everything pertaining
to life and godliness, through the true knowledge
of Him who called us by His own glory and excellence.*

2 PETER 1:3

Demons thrive in chaos, but God brings a steady, secure equilibrium to the lives of people in covenant with Him through Jesus Christ. Old sailing ships often carried lead to provide ballast. God provides the ballast for our lives—moral excellence, knowledge, self-control, perseverance, godliness, brotherly kindness, and love (vs. 5–7). Without such weight, the craft of your life can be capsized by contrary waves and winds. God's promise is that as, by faith, you add these things to your life in Christian growth, you are strengthening the ballast that will hold you upright in a hurricane.

May 19

For by these He has granted to us His precious and magnificent promises, so that by them you may become partakers of the divine nature, having escaped the corruption that is in the world by lust.

2 PETER 1:4

Siring means sharing. In fathering a child, a man passes on the essence of himself, while recognizing the child will have his distinct ways. All humans are created by God, but sin separated us from His character. In the salvation covenant through Christ, the Creator becomes *Abba* Father— "Dad." The new birth means we participate in God's very nature. The moment each of my sons came into the world, my home, food, and resources were theirs. So when we are born into God's Kingdom through Jesus Christ, all His promises are ours, by inheritance.

May 20

My God will supply all your needs
according to His riches in glory in Christ Jesus.

PHILIPPIANS 4:19

Indignation and protest twist through contemporary culture like choking vines. "Can't anyone understand who I am? I've got legitimate needs. Doesn't anyone care?" go the plaints of the angry. But if we live by the promises of God we don't get upset when other people ignore our needs. Our supply doesn't come from them, but from God. An unhealthy codependence occurs when our happiness depends upon how others view and treat us. Drawing on God's supply delivers us from preoccupation with our needs and anger with people who seem to fail to recognize them.

*For you know the grace of our Lord Jesus Christ, that
though He was rich, yet for your sake He became poor,
so that you through His poverty might become rich.*

2 CORINTHIANS 8:9

What we consider as riches tells a lot about us.
A friend visited Mother Teresa's House for
the Dying in Calcutta. She asked a helper, "How do
you stand doing this day after day?" The woman
pointed to a portrait of Jesus, with the caption, *My
Lord and my God.* "He is not only my Lord and my
God, but He has given me the privilege to be here
His hands, eyes, mind and feet. I count it a privilege,"
The woman said. The little lady ministering to
Calcutta's dying was more joyful in her wealth of
opportunity than moguls in their mammon.

May 22

God arms me with strength; he has made my way safe.

PSALM 18:32 NLT

Weather has determined the outcome of many battles. It was frustration with hampering conditions that prompted General George Patton to ask his chaplain to write and issue a "weather prayer" two days before the Battle of the Bulge. The Allies won by air power, made possible by fair weather. David, God's anointed, had skirmished and fought many foes. King Saul sought his life. But whenever David seemed outnumbered and overwhelmed, God would somehow get him through the fog and storm. God's covenant promise is that He will make conditions right for victory for you.

May 23

*Therefore, brethren, since we have confidence
to enter the holy place by the blood of Jesus, . . .
a great priest over the house of God, let us draw
near with a sincere heart in full assurance of faith,
having our hearts sprinkled clean from an evil
conscience and our bodies washed with pure water.*

HEBREWS 10:19, 22

Before he became a pastor, an associate served as
an aide to the president. My colleague knew the
thrill of getting his White House pass, granting
access to the Oval Office itself. Jesus' blood is our
pass into the very presence of the Most High. When
we arrive, we discover Jesus is the High Priest—
in charge. My associate lost his White House pass
when he resigned, and he jokes that he can't even go
near the door now. But because we are in Christ,
and because His blood is the pass, we never lose our
access and can always go there with confidence.

O people in Zion, inhabitant in Jerusalem, you will weep no longer. He will surely be gracious to you at the sound of your cry; when He hears it, He will answer you.

ISAIAH 30:19

P arents today have intercoms they can place near a baby's crib. No matter where they are in the house, mom and dad can respond to the slightest whimper. God listens intently to the cries of His people. He heard the groaning of the Hebrews in Egypt's slave camps, remembered His covenants of promise, and set them free (Exodus 2:24–25). So when sin's shackles rub you raw, when temptation snarls in your path, when trials bring you to desperation, and you cry out, you discover He is gracious.

May 25

Therefore, having been justified by faith,
we have peace with God through our Lord Jesus Christ,
through whom also we have obtained our
introduction by faith into this grace in which we stand;
and we exult in hope of the glory of God.

ROMANS 5:1-2

What's your excuse?" the indignant boss demands when the project deadline is missed. Someday the Judge will ask you why you fell short of His glory. The besieged employee tells the boss she had to attend her dying mother and is justified in the eyes of the merciful supervisor. At the Judgment Seat, all we need reply is "Jesus," and we are instantly justified. A pastor I know preached the funeral of an evil man who had accepted Christ right before death. The pastor focused on Christ's mercy. "What you said," a man told him later, "is that Jesus was his excuse."

164

May 26

He will be like a tree firmly planted by streams of water,
Which yields its fruit in its season
And its leaf does not wither;
And in whatever he does, he prospers.

PSALM 1:3

God's covenant people aren't accidental sprouts, but *planted* trees. Planting means purpose. The spot is chosen carefully, near a stream. The waters' edge is where we grow best. You may have been born in adversity to learn how to overcome. But always the waters are nearby. There is a place where you best hear and respond to the Holy Spirit. God will plant you there. Your purpose is to bear fruit—the fruit of the Kingdom harvest, the fruit of repentance, and the fruit of the Spirit. But no water, no fruit. God knows where to plant you. Receive your place with gladness.

May 27

*"I am the LORD, I have called You in righteousness,
I will also hold You by the hand and watch over You,
And I will appoint You as a covenant to the people,
As a light to the nations."*

ISAIAH 42:6

A New Guinea native attended a missions conference in Singapore. He had never seen a city and was amazed at the "long buildings." But he was terrified by the rushing traffic. One day he was crossing the street with a conference participant who worked in urban areas. The man from New Guinea hesitated at the curb. The city missionary took him by the hand. "When I come to your jungle, you will hold my hand to help me. When you come to my jungle, I will hold your hand and help you." God holds our hands through life's jungles.

May 28

*"Peace I leave with you; My peace I give to you;
not as the world gives do I give to you. Do not let your
heart be troubled, nor let it be fearful."*

JOHN 14:27

E d, our oldest son, now a pastor in Dallas, was born while Jo Beth and I served in a small North Carolina textile community. A midwife stayed with us. She was a godly woman, so one Thursday, desperate for a preaching topic, I asked her, "What's the best sermon you ever heard?" "It was on 'heart trouble,'" she replied. "What was the text?" I asked. "John 14!" she answered. We may be focused on physical heart trouble, but God's concern is that the spiritual heart not be troubled. If it is well, our whole being will be untroubled.

May 29

*"For I, the Son of Man, will come in the glory
of my Father with his angels and
will judge all people according to their deeds."*

MATTHEW 16:27 NLT

Deeds fall into three categories. One is "brick deeds." These evil acts layer into a high tower. We glory in the height of our works, only to find they are also our judgment as they come crashing down on us in the earthquake of God's wrath. Then there are "kindling deeds." Everything we lay on the foundation of Christ that does not honor and point people to Him is burned up (1 Corinthians 3:12, 15). The third is the "investment deeds." These are the enduring treasures we lay up in Heaven (Matthew 6:20) which determine our rewards in eternity.

Many are the sorrows of the wicked,
But he who trusts in the LORD,
lovingkindness shall surround him.

PSALM 32:10

Noise is the nagging companion that stalks us everywhere. Music drones in waiting rooms and thuds in restaurants where dishes clatter and orders are shouted. At home the TV blares, phones ring, doors slam, pets yelp. It makes one yearn for a cone of silence. That day when an adulterous woman was brought to Jesus, the accusing religious herd was silenced suddenly. "Let the one who has no sin throw the first stone," He said (John 8:7). Sounds of dropping stones and scampering feet replaced growling voices; then there was silence. The Prince of Peace had surrounded her with lovingkindness.

*"Every branch in Me that does not bear fruit,
He takes away; and every branch that bears fruit,
He prunes it so that it may bear more fruit."*

JOHN 15:2

Religion is *doing* with the hope it will lead to spiritual being. Life in Christ is *being* that leads to doing. Religion is "do's" and "don'ts," but life in Christ is being attached to Him, like a branch to a tree. As long as the branch is linked to the tree, fruit happens. Branches don't do self-pruning. The husbandman—the farmer—does the hacking. Our mission is to abide in Christ. When something in us is not bearing fruit, God will reveal it as we pray and study His Word. Then we submit to His pruning through repentance, and He lops off our fruitless twigs.

June

June 1

"I will betroth you to Me forever;
Yes, I will betroth you to Me in righteousness and in justice,
In lovingkindness and in compassion,
And I will betroth you to Me in faithfulness.
Then you will know the LORD."

HOSEA 2:19-20

Until death do us part." Multitudes of couples have uttered those words to one another. But somewhere along the way, their memories suggested they had said, "Until *debt* do us part," or, "Until *emotions* do us part." When God enters relationship with His covenant people, we are "married" to Him forever. Ancient Jewish men could write their wives a certificate of divorce, putting her out for the most minor infraction, even if it was only in the husband's eyes. God *never* scribbles a bill of divorce. Not even death parts us from Him. In fact, death only takes us into deeper intimacy and joy.

June 2

"For You are my lamp, O LORD;
And the LORD illumines my darkness."

2 SAMUEL 22:29

There is a darkness that is all yours. It is the stifling cloak of guilt, or the cavern of private fears, or the abyss of confusion. Visitors to Carlsbad Caverns in New Mexico reach a point deep underground when the guide tells everyone to be seated and then turns off the lights. The darkness is so complete, people can't even see their hands an inch from their eyes. One match seems a torch. Not only does Jesus Christ drive the darkness from the cosmos, but He illumines *my* darkness— and *yours*, if you are in covenant with Him through Christ.

June 3

How blessed are those who observe His testimonies,
Who seek Him with all their heart.

PSALM 119:2

G et serious." That's an admonition to people who take things lightly. Jesus' mission was to make disciples, learners who will take Him and His Kingdom with seriousness. Popular cultural religion often degenerates to a casual item of curiosity. But there's a proportionate relationship between experiencing God's blessings and taking Him seriously. Those who treasure His ways and search Him out to follow Him—to become His disciples— enter a zone of joy and strength.

June 4

"You will receive power when the Holy Spirit
has come upon you; and you shall be My witnesses
both in Jerusalem, and in all Judea and Samaria,
and even to the remotest part of the earth."

ACTS 1:8

Jesus' promise to His disciples stands throughout
history. Acts 2 reports that His followers went
back to Jerusalem, as He commanded, and that the
Holy Spirit empowered them, creating the church.
When you and I received Christ, we came into
that anointing—or baptism—with the Spirit, and
have an anointing that remains (1 John 2:27).
Eons ago, the great furnace at the heart of the sun
ignited, and all born into this world universe bathe
in its energy. Two thousand years ago, the fire of
the church was set ablaze, and to be born into
Christ is to come into this baptism of fire.

June 5

Those who live in his shadow
Will again raise grain,
And they will blossom like the vine.
His renown will be like the wine of Lebanon.

HOSEA 14:7

Wing trouble caused a creative angel to dump the rocks he was to spread over the earth on just one place instead—the land we know now as Israel. That's the way an old legend describes it. The Land of Promise was full of fertile plains, but also of rocky wastelands. Yet even in those inhospitable places, the Hebrews raised grain and grape vines. God's promise to His people is that those dependent on Him will have nourishment and vitality, even in life's dry deserts.

June 6

*No temptation has overtaken you but such as
is common to man; and God is faithful, who will not
allow you to be tempted beyond what you are able,
but with the temptation will provide the way of escape
also, so that you will be able to endure it.*

1 CORINTHIANS 10:13

A test becomes a temptation when we internalize it. The Garden's fruit dangled before Adam and Eve daily. But when they began listening to the serpent and contemplating their own perversion of God's good creation, the Tree of Life became temptation to them. God's promise is that He knows your limits. He sees inside you and won't allow you to be pressed to the breaking point, if you're in covenant with Him. God tempts no one with evil (James 1:13). If testing becomes temptation, we can overcome it by setting our minds on things above (Colossians 3:2).

June 7

For the mind set on the flesh is death,
but the mind set on the Spirit is life and peace.

ROMANS 8:6

Are you a "springer" or a "feeler"? Springers pop out of bed each morning ready to dance into the day. Feelers take it slow. Their eyes open and they lie there awhile, then stretch one leg down to the floor, followed slowly by the other. I know, because I'm a feeler. Springers also go to sleep when their heads hit the pillow. But we feelers ease in and ease out. When I ease into the day after waking, I am setting my mind, a necessity for both types. If you're a springer, it's important to discipline yourself to wait and set your mind on the Spirit, and if you're a feeler, you must discipline yourself out of bed once the mind is set.

June 8

Those who love Your law have great peace,
And nothing causes them to stumble.

PSALM 119:165

Some years ago I took a painful fall while jogging through Houston's Memorial Park. My problem was that I relaxed my focus on the path to speak to another runner. Before I knew it, I had stumbled and thudded to the ground, gashing my head and face. As we move through the world, it's vital we keep our eyes on God's path. If we do that, we need not fear stumbling. For the ancient Jews, that meant constant observance of the Law. But in the New Covenant, watching the path means keep our eyes on our Forerunner, Jesus Christ.

June 9

For in the day of trouble He will conceal me
in His tabernacle;
In the secret place of His tent He will hide me;
He will lift me up on a rock.

PSALM 27:5

Usually we wouldn't think of a tent as being secure. The key is found in who is in the tent. If the occupant is more powerful than the assaulting enemy, the tent is secure. God chose to manifest His presence among His covenant people upon the Mercy Seat, atop the Ark of the Covenant. As the Hebrews passed through the wilderness, they housed the Ark in the Tabernacle. The tent's walls were of cloth, but its content was the Almighty God. If you are in Christ's covenant, you dwell in the tent of His presence, and you are safe there, no matter where you go.

June 10

*For judgment will be merciless to one who
has shown no mercy; mercy triumphs over judgment.*

JAMES 2:13

A man told me he had read the Bible and had decided to show mercy to everyone, certain that God then would be merciful to him in judgment. But it doesn't work that way. Mercy isn't a savings account. You don't accumulate "credits" that God pays you in eternity. Mercy is a state of being that comes from Christ's indwelling presence within you. A lack of mercy would suggest Christ's character is not being formed in a person, and that he or she doesn't know Him. The mercy you may show others demonstrates Christ's influence on your life.

June 11

[The righteous] will not fear evil tidings;
His heart is steadfast, trusting in the LORD.

PSALM 112:7

News junkies constitute a whole class of people in our media-saturated culture. Sometimes it seems 99.9 percent of the news coming at us daily is bad. But God's promise to His covenant people is that they don't have to fear evil tidings. That doesn't mean they are exempt from dread phone calls or other alarming information. However, God's covenant people don't have to exist in a perpetual state of anxiety. Down deep inside they trust in God, and they know He works all things for good and His glory in their lives.

June 12

The weapons of our warfare are not of the flesh,
but divinely powerful for the destruction of fortresses.

2 CORINTHIANS 10:4

Jail inmates dream of freedom. The sudden thump of a wrecking ball knocking down the walls would be happy music to their ears. Multitudes of people are jailed behind massive walls that aren't physical, but spiritual, emotional, and mental. They are locked into addictions and behaviors that limit them as much as the strongest prison bars. The walls of such fortresses can't be knocked down by physical powers, but God's covenant people have spiritual weapons through Jesus Christ that no fortress can hold back.

June 13

*For the commandment is a lamp
and the teaching is light;
And reproofs for discipline are the way of life.*

PROVERBS 6:23

Lamps and light are designed for one another. Take the light from the lamp and there's only a cold, dark structure. Take the lamp from the light, and there can be the devastation of uncontained, uncontrolled fire. But put the lamp and light together, and there is illumination. God's commandments constitute the structure for the light. The fire in the lamp is the content of the lamp and provides its meaning. When Jesus comes He does not destroy the Law, for to do so would be to shatter the lamp. Rather, He comes to provide the fire that gives meaning to the lamp.

The LORD is near to all who call upon Him,
To all who call upon Him in truth.

PSALM 145:18

Parents of adult children sometimes are reluctant to initiate contacts, fearing they will intrude. Yet they yearn for interaction. There's a thrill when the phone rings or they hear a friendly tap on the door. God isn't an intruder, and He loves answering the calls and the door-knocks of His covenant children. The Bible says we are to wait on the Lord, but He waits on us, too. Some people believe they shouldn't bother God. They forget He is Father, and wants to hear from His children.

June 15

Anxiety in a man's heart weighs it down,
But a good word makes it glad.

PROVERBS 12:25

The best of experts may not be able to tell you precisely what it means when a person says, "I'm tired." Some might say tiredness is depletion of energy. Such a problem can be cured with an infusion of strength. Anxiety saps us, but a positive, encouraging word replenishes the emotions. There is no greater means of regaining energy than a "fill-up" with God's Word—the best of all. "God loves you," "God cares for you," connect with the regenerated human spirit and overflow outward into the mind and emotions, stirring gladness.

June 16

"He who listens to me shall live securely
And will be at ease from the dread of evil."

PROVERBS 1:33

To merely hear is to experience sound waves on the eardrum. To listen is to absorb the content of a message. A pet may hear sounds, but it perks up its ears at the voice of the master. The individual who draws close to God to listen has two promises. First, she can live with confidence in the knowledge that God is her constant companion. Second, she is able to rest in the turbulence of the fallen world. God's promises, really heeded, become the consuming focus of the mind, not the jarring noises and voices of a world gone wild. Perk up your ears.

June 17

"He will exult over you with joy,
He will be quiet in His love,
He will rejoice over you with shouts of joy."

ZEPHANIAH 3:17

God's love for you spans the range of emotions from quiet contemplation to an exuberant "hoorah!" Sin kidnapped you and held you hostage. God fully paid the ransom through the cross. When you are restored to Him through Jesus Christ, His joy makes the stars of heaven dance. He's like a father on a big holiday with all the family around him. He lavishes his eyes on the feast of his children's presence. Your heavenly Father rejoices in your presence, and the key to your joy is being with Him.

June 18

The testing of your faith produces endurance.

JAMES 1:3

Shaken to the roots." That's an expression describing a person going through a severe crisis. But nature teaches that the tree most severely impacted by the storm puts down the deepest roots. Branches may be snapped off, twigs broken, and leaves ripped away, but deep roots are undisturbed by the howling gales. In fact, they only get deeper and stronger. Your existence is like the tree trunk, up in the tumult. But if you are in Christ, your life is hidden in its roots, which the storms can't touch.

June 19

Now to the one who works, his wage is not credited as a favor, but as what is due. But to the one who does not work, but believes in Him who justifies the ungodly, his faith is credited as righteousness.

ROMANS 4:4-5

A favorite *I Love Lucy* episode depicts Lucy Ricardo trying to box chocolates from a speeding conveyer belt. Many laborers do piece work, and are paid by the number of items they produce or process. They get their due wages based on their work. God's righteousness is absolute and only 100 percent purity meets His quota. But God's mercy is also absolute; therefore, He makes provision to satisfy the requirements of His justice. You can't do enough piece work to satisfy God's expectations, so He takes care of them for you, through Jesus Christ. That's the wonderful promise of His grace.

June 20

Now the God of peace, who brought up from the dead the great Shepherd of the sheep through the blood of the eternal covenant, even Jesus our Lord, equip you in every good thing to do His will, working in us that which is pleasing in His sight, through Jesus Christ, to whom be the glory forever and ever. Amen.

HEBREWS 13:20–21

While our works are inadequate to earn our way to Heaven, once we know and love the Lord, we want to serve Him. We no longer strive to be good enough; instead, we rest in His grace and work because it's our heart's desire. Then we plug into the promise of His provision. My city, Houston, sends expatriates to work in the world's oilfields. Their companies supply all they need to sustain quality of life and perform the tasks in those remote places. When you work for the Kingdom, God equips you with everything you need to get the job done.

June 21

Submit yourselves for the Lord's sake to every human institution, whether to a king as the one in authority, or to governors as sent by him for the punishment of evildoers and the praise of those who do right. For such is the will of God that by doing right you may silence the ignorance of foolish men.

1 PETER 2:13–15

Chaos is the aim of the Destroyer. Satan seeks to take apart everything God puts together. God grants authority to restrain the disorder. Human governments mediate God's authority. When they rebel from His order, they become subject to overthrow. But God's covenant people have the assignment of submitting to true authority. The foolish are those who seek to lead rebellion, only for the sake of seizing power. God's promise is that as His people submit to God-granted authority, they help squelch the rebellious and maintain society's peace.

June 22

Do not let kindness and truth leave you;
Bind them around your neck,
Write them on the tablet of your heart.
So you will find favor and good repute
In the sight of God and man.

PROVERBS 3:3–4

I f you have tenderness toward God, you will be tender toward others. Among the greatest blessings a wife can have is a kind husband—and vice versa. But such behavior arises from a heart that has first experienced and interacted with the kindness of God. Truth and kindness must be held in balance. Kind people must be willing to tell the truth, and truth-focused individuals must speak the facts kindly. Such a balance leads to blessing in a home and in all other life endeavors.

June 23

"I did not come to judge the world, but to save the world."

JOHN 12:47

Many people prefer an indifferent God. They have concluded wrongly that God's greatest delight is to condemn them. The New Age Movement of the late twentieth century taught that people could access this impersonal "force" through channeling, meditation, crystals, and other means. Eastern mysticism—a continuation of ancient Gnosticism—tries to position people "properly" in relation to the spiritual dimension. The Bible gives us the true picture: God loves, He cares, and He engages with us, not to condemn us but to save us.

June 24

*For the LORD God is a sun and shield;
The LORD gives grace and glory;
No good thing does He withhold from
those who walk uprightly.*

PSALM 84:11

If God is love, if He cares, if He is engaged with us, it is illogical to believe He will hide what He intends for us. Yet many think God is capricious and enjoys seeing us sweat. They have mistaken the Greek gods for the true and living God. God has purpose and plan for every life, and He provides a North Star to help us move toward our destiny. It contradicts logic as well as biblical revelation to think that God-Who-Is-Love would withhold any good thing from the people who desire His will above all else.

Therefore, my beloved brethren, be steadfast, immovable, always abounding in the work of the Lord, knowing that your toil is not in vain in the Lord.

1 CORINTHIANS 15:58

God can do anything He desires, but He has chosen humans to be His co-laborers. It takes God's provision and an individual's toil to produce the harvest. Without God, we can do nothing. Without our effort and cooperation, God won't accomplish His aims. This is not because He is weak, but because He is faithful to His covenant. God appointed Adam and Eve to tend the Garden, and the Garden would supply what they needed. This covenant of provision and performance stands. And the guarantee is that whatever we do in and through God will always bear fruit.

June 26

*It is God who is at work in you, both to will
and to work for His good pleasure.*

PHILIPPIANS 2:13

"Go with your feelings" is the philosophy by which
many guide their lives. The only time you can
trust your feelings is when you know you are under
Christ's Lordship, seeking His Kingdom above all.
Willing comes before *doing.* When your soul is
piloted by the Holy Spirit, He is also the navigator,
directing the course through creating in you the
will to do what the Father desires. If you are in
covenant with God through Jesus Christ, and His
Kingdom is your passion, note the desires He
creates in you, and go with His flow for your life.

June 27

> *"'You will seek Me and find Me when you
> search for Me with all your heart.'"*

JEREMIAH 29:13

Just follow your heart, and you can't go wrong." People offering that advice don't understand that "the heart is more deceitful than all else" (Jeremiah 17:9). However, when the focus of the heart is the quest for God, then the heart leads in the right direction. God is love, and He wants to be found. He doesn't conceal Himself in an attempt to avoid us. Rather, He wants us to desire Him as He desires us. Seeking and searching for Him is looking for *His* heart. When a person's heart seeks and searches for God's heart, discovery is guaranteed.

June 28

"I am with you always, even to the end of the age."
MATTHEW 28:20

C hrist's followers have an assignment and a promise to the end of the age. The assignment is to penetrate the world with Christ's Gospel. The promise is that of His enduring presence all the way. He is with us in two ways: objectively and manifestly. His objective presence is the *promise of the presence*, and His manifest presence is the *presence of the promise*. He is with us because He promised He would be. Yet Christ's manifest presence comes as we experience His nearness, or see some tangible expression of His power. The objective presence reassures us and the manifest presence transforms us.

June 29

I know that everything God does will remain forever.

ECCLESIASTES 3:14

Most of us get our names in the newspaper twice—when we are born and when we die. However, there's no obituary for the works of God. The human mind reels at the thought. We are three-dimensional beings who must have boundaries, points of termination. We cannot conceive of infinity. Yet the human spirit, as the work of God, is eternal. To be separated from God by sin is to live through the endless spans beyond time without Him. Hell can be no worse than that. But to become God's special work through Jesus Christ is to remain forever with Him whose work remains forever.

June 30

In this is love, not that we loved God, but that He loved us and sent His Son to be the propitiation for our sins.

1 JOHN 4:10

When Nixon aide Chuck Colson was convicted of Watergate-related crimes, his family was already in crisis, and Colson grieved over being removed from them to serve prison time. Colson had recently become a Christian, and he was one of a group of other government officials who followed Christ. A high-level government executive in the group actually offered to serve Colson's time in prison. The law wouldn't allow it. But it was a different case when Christ presented Himself to take your penalty and mine. God permitted His Son to take the death sentence that sin had imposed on us. He became our substitute and took on our sentence.

July

July 1

When it goes well with the righteous, the city rejoices.

PROVERBS 11:10

God's people are blessing bearers. Noah found favor in God's eyes, and his whole family was spared. Abraham knew that if a mere five righteous men could be found in Sodom, the city would escape God's judgment. Joseph was sold into slavery in Potiphar's house in Egypt, and consequently the Lord's blessing was on all Potiphar's property (Genesis 39:5). The presence of Christ-redeemed people in a society bear God's blessings into their city and nation. There is a direct link between their well-being and the vitality of the social and political units of which they are a part.

July 2

By the blessing of the upright a city is exalted.

PROVERBS 11:11

William Bradford and the Mayflower Pilgrims dreamed of a society that would be like a "city on a hill," setting an example for all the world of what a nation would like under God's Kingdom. They brought that ideal into what would become America. History's freest and most prosperous nation was born, not in Philadelphia's Constitution Hall, not in the debates between the Federalists and the Anti-Federalists, not even on the Yorktown battlefield, but in the hearts of the upright people who wanted to establish a society that would glorify God.

July 3

Truthful lips will be established forever,
But a lying tongue is only for a moment.

PROVERBS 12:19

Free societies stand or fall on the way they handle truth. Politicians who lie to the people ultimately are discovered and lose their ability to lead. Trust is vital for the democratic process. Without God and His absolute truth, political systems determine their own standards and change them at will. One communist-era dissenter wrote that truth was whatever the state declared it to be at the moment.[14] God's truth, revealed in His Word, is established forever, and upholds individuals, families, and their institutions, no matter what.

July 4

Blessed is the nation whose God is the LORD,
The people whom He has chosen for His own inheritance.

PSALM 33:12

Frederick the Great supposedly asked his chaplain for a simple proof of God's existence. "The Jews," the chaplain responded. I would include America. I was disturbed as a young history major that what we learn from history is that we seem never to learn from history, to paraphrase one scholar. When God is Lord of a nation, her values reflect His character, her culture reverences Him, and her leaders submit to Him as Supreme Sovereign. As long as a nation places itself under the true God, revealed in the Bible, she is blessed. America proves it. We must relearn that historic principle or lose the blessing.

*"Blessed are the poor in spirit,
for theirs is the kingdom of heaven."*

MATTHEW 5:3

Eleven-year olds in British schools were to be taught lessons in happiness through a curriculum designed by an American guru to reduce "a huge rise in depression, self-harm, and anti-social behaviour" among the young.[15] But happiness is a byproduct of a state of being called "joy," the fruit of the Holy Spirit. The "poor in spirit" recognize that self-made happy potions can't help them, that they are empty and depleted apart from God. Jesus has no good news for "rich in spirit," only for those so impoverished they know they need Him.

"Blessed are those who mourn, for they shall be comforted."

MATTHEW 5:4

Every virtue needs correction by its opposite virtue. A jungle flower in the East Indian tropics smells putrid alone, but mingled with the other forest scents it's pleasant. So some virtues taken by themselves can "smell bad." Denunciation in spirit, recognizing that one is bankrupt at the core of their life ends in lonely asceticism unless balanced by engagement with the world. Such involvement will lead to mourning because of the pain in the fallen societies. But it's those who grieve over the sorrow brought by evil who wind up with God's dearest comfort.

July 7

"*Blessed are the gentle, for they shall inherit the earth.*"

MATTHEW 5:5

Gentleness, or meekness, refers not to wimpiness but to discipline, as in a strong horse under control. There is also another implication. In French, Jesus' saying could be translated, "Blessed are the *debonair.*" This describes the person who doesn't succumb to pettiness, who is above a spiteful, small-spirited attitude. Such disciplined and gracious people may seem pushed aside in the short-term, but at the end of the day, they are the real winners.

*"Blessed are those who hunger and
thirst for righteousness, for they shall be satisfied."*

MATTHEW 5:6

The U. S. government maintains a Bureau of Standards, Weights and Measures to help people keep scales set right and rulers accurate. God's character is the "rightness," the standard for everything in the universe. The most successful employees in a business are those who pay attention to the details and passionately work to get things right. The people in the world who have the greatest yearning to see everything line up with God's character are those who will be satisfied. Someday there will be a new heaven and a new earth, completely aligned with God's holiness.

"Blessed are the merciful, for they shall receive mercy."

MATTHEW 5:7

O ptimists teach their kids the Golden Rule, but pessimists grouse that if you're kind to others they'll just kick you in the face. The lack of civility has become a problem in our culture as more people embrace the pessimists than the optimists. But God's people align with Christ, no matter how wavering the bright-siders, nor how glum the nay-sayers. Jesus doesn't merely command mercy; He attaches a promise. We don't look for reciprocity from other people. The mercy Christ's followers receive comes from God, the Judge of the universe.

July 10

"Blessed are the pure in heart, for they shall see God."

MATTHEW 5:8

T o adulterate is to contaminate. "Adultery" describes sexual sin, but "adulteration" is even broader. It leads to weakness and eventually disintegration. Adultery in pagan Greece and Rome was punishable by death, as it was in Old Testament Israel. So adulteration of soul and spirit—like physical adultery—leads to a separation from fellowship with God. Some married people have affairs because they think they will be happy. But the pure in spirit know the happiness that springs from the joy of walking in uninterrupted communion with God.

"*Blessed are the peacemakers,
for they shall be called sons of God.*"

MATTHEW 5:9

As Jesus spoke, Galilee stretched out from the hillside like a pit full of Rottweilers, all snarling at one another. Nobody liked, trusted, or got along with anyone else. Anyone suggesting peacemakers would be blessed sounded like they were from another planet—or kingdom. *And Jesus was.* He brought the values of the Kingdom of Heaven into the fallen kingdoms of the world. Conflict-stirrers were the admired, hair-triggers the expected, but Jesus says peacemakers will be called the children of God.

July 12

"Blessed are those who have been persecuted for the sake of righteousness, for theirs is the kingdom of heaven."

MATTHEW 5:10

To understand the bliss of persecution, it's important to note the difference between *punishment* and persecution. Punishment is given by good people for evil deeds. Persecution is meted out by evil people against the good. Therefore, when you are harassed and maltreated because of your commitment to Christ, you can be happy that you are honored to be identified with Him. Paul wrote that "all who desire to live godly in Christ Jesus will be persecuted" (2 Timothy 3:12). Self-righteousness might earn you punishment, but identification with Christ's righteousness will get you persecuted. And that's a badge of honor.

July 13

*"Blessed are you when people insult you
and persecute you, and falsely say all kinds of evil
against you because of Me. Rejoice and be glad,
for your reward in heaven is great."*

MATTHEW 5:11-12

Today, Christians may not be hurled into the coliseums to face hungry lions, but we are cast into the chronicles of daily media. The spin machines of ancient Rome depicted Christians as unpatriotic cannibals who drank blood at "love feasts." Today's spinners write, as did one in *The Washington Post,* that Christians are "uneducated and easily led."[16] Such is no surprise to the followers of the Man Who was regarded by the establishment elite twenty centuries ago as a rabble rouser from the boondocks. When people spread rumors and lies about you it's time to rejoice—they have linked you with your Master.

July 14

*"Bring the whole tithe into the storehouse,
so that there may be food in My house, and test Me
now in this," says the LORD of hosts, "if I will not
open for you the windows of heaven and pour out
for you a blessing until it overflows."*

MALACHI 3:10

Blessed nations are giving nations. The tithe is the *first* tenth of one's income. The "firstfruits" principle is all through the Bible, from Abel and his gift of the first and best of his harvest (Genesis 4:4), to God's command to the Promised Land–bound Hebrews to set apart their firstborn sons (Exodus 13:2), to the Proverbs admonition to honor the Lord with the firstfruits (3:9). The "storehouse" in Malachi's day was the Temple. Now, it is the local church. When God's people honor Him with firstfruits giving, there is a radiating effect outward to society itself, resulting in generosity and blessing.

July 15

Christ redeemed us from the curse of the Law, having become a curse for us—for it is written, "CURSED IS EVERYONE WHO HANGS ON A TREE"—in order that in Christ Jesus the blessing of Abraham might come to the Gentiles, so that we would receive the promise of the Spirit through faith.

GALATIANS 3:13-14

Board a fancy cruise ship and all the amenities are yours—the fine food, sparkling floor shows, elegant lounges. Centuries ago, God promised Abraham that the seed "in" him would be blessed beyond imagination. Then the focus narrowed to one Jew who came through Abraham's line—Jesus Christ. Through Him, the most amazing thing happens: Non-Jews, Gentiles, have opportunity to become one with the marvelous covenant God made with Abraham. Get in Christ, and all the amenities of the covenant are yours.

July 16

How blessed is the man who does not walk
in the counsel of the wicked,
Nor stand in the path of sinners,
Nor sit in the seat of scoffers!

PSALM 1:1

Happy is the person who doesn't walk by the counsel of people whose lives have no reference to God. Blessed is the individual who doesn't stand with those who miss God's mark. Happy is the man or woman who doesn't "sit a spell" with cynics. To enjoy the promise of God's blessing, we must be careful where we walk, stand, and sit. Behavior, alignment, and fellowship are points on the compass leading to happiness or misery.

July 17

*How blessed is the man to whom the LORD
does not impute iniquity,
And in whose spirit there is no deceit!*

PSALM 32:2

For many people, there is no greater relief than paying off a thirty-year mortgage. Perhaps a homeowner's mind journeys back to the day she signed the sheath of loan papers and the anxiety she felt as she left the mortgage company with all that debt hanging over her. But then comes the joy of the loan being paid in full. The sin-debt is the heaviest, most pressing a person will ever know. Its principle is impossibly high, and it is paid, not monthly, but moment by moment. God's grace means payment of the debt in full. With His own blood, Jesus Christ wrote the check that paid off the mortgage.

O taste and see that the LORD is good;
How blessed is the man who takes refuge in Him!

PSALM 34:8

Jo Beth and I went to seminary in North Carolina right after getting married. We had no place to live and were almost penniless. Then we met a woman who rented log cabins. The cold mountain wind pierced through in the winter and spiders frequented it in the summer. God gave Jo Beth a job, and soon we were able to rent a house. It was a small duplex, but to us it was a castle. Refuge is a precious thing when you know what it means to be exposed. God's promise is that when you are in covenant with Him, you dwell in Him. He caulks the rafters and plugs the holes and covers you with a roof. You can rest at last.

July 19

How blessed is he who considers the helpless;
The LORD will deliver him in a day of trouble.

PSALM 41:1

It's satisfying to help someone get on their feet.
I was barely twenty-four when I became pastor
of a church in Erwin, North Carolina. The people
in that mill village helped me get on my feet. They
taught me and built things into my life that help
me stand today. Floyd Glover, Erin Holmes, Roy
Godwin, and a host of others bring happiness to
my heart just thinking of their names. They also
have a big share in any successes I enjoy, because
Jo Beth and I were helpless, and they considered us
enough to be patient and serve the young pastor
who thought he had come to serve them.

July 20

How blessed is the one whom
You choose and bring near to You
To dwell in Your courts.
We will be satisfied with the goodness of Your house,
Your holy temple.

PSALM 65:4

Marie Antoinette, wife of France's King Louis XVI, was surrounded by her court. When she traveled to her summer palace, a whole train of wagons followed, loaded with the courtiers. No peasant would ever be selected to attend the queen. But when the God of the universe chooses those who will dwell in His courts, only the humble qualify. Earthly potentates gather in the elites. The King of kings brings around Him the lowly. That's why if you are exalted, He in His mercy will humble you. He invites you to dwell in His courts.

July 21

How blessed is the man whose strength is in You,
In whose heart are the highways to Zion!

PSALM 84:5

Happiness is in knowing where you're going and having strength for the journey. Young Anglican ministers in colonial America had to go to England for ordination. In the six-month roundtrip, some were depleted and gave up, missing their life mission. Jim DeLoach, now in his fifth decade of ministry, has had a long journey. I've known and worked with him most of those years, and I can testify that the "highways to Zion" were in his heart from the beginning. God has given him strength to stay on the road, and Jim has led many others on that highway, and he manifests the joy God promised.

July 22

How blessed are the people who know the joyful sound!
O LORD, they walk in the light of Your countenance.

PSALM 89:15

When I was a schoolboy coming home in the afternoon, my mother would be in the tiny kitchen of our small house. And she would be singing. "In the morning I see His face; in the evening His form I trace; in the darkness His voice in know. I see Jesus everywhere." That joyful sound hasn't left me, and it still brings me happiness these decades later. But there's something even better—the joyful sound of God's voice accompanied by the praises of His people. That will light you up every time.

How blessed are those who keep justice,
Who practice righteousness at all times!

PSALM 106:3

Practice makes perfect. Practicing righteousness is a strange phenomenon. The moment a person receives Jesus Christ as Savior, he or she is justified and declared "perfect" (Hebrews 10:14). Yet the practice of righteousness moves one toward perfection. How can you progress toward what you already have? The covenant person lives on two levels—Heaven and earth. In Heaven, to be in Christ is to have already arrived in His perfection. Practicing righteousness in the earthly life is moving toward the state of being one already possesses in Heaven.

July 24

How blessed is the man who fears the LORD,
Who greatly delights in His commandments.
His descendants will be mighty on earth;
The generation of the upright will be blessed.

PSALM 112:1-2

Some sociologists say there's a five-generation rule in the raising of children. The way you bring up your child impacts not only him or her, but the four generations that follow.[17] Princeton scholar Benjamin Warfield tested the rule by comparing descendants of godly Jonathan Edwards to those of atheist Max Jukes. Edwards's progeny included 13 college presidents, 65 professors, 30 judges, 100 lawyers, 60 physicians and 100 pastors. Jukes's descendants numbered 310 paupers, 150 criminals, seven murderers and more than 100 alcoholics.[18] Happiness is on the side of those who reverence God.

July 25

How blessed are those whose way is blameless,
Who walk in the law of the LORD.

PSALM 119:1

Freedom is obedience to the law," read an inscription on a courthouse. "That quotation is incorrect!" said a visiting judge. He knew the sixteenth-century British theologian Thomas Hooker was the source, and that what Hooker really said was, "Of Law there can be no less acknowledged than that her seat is the bosom of God, her voice the harmony of the world."[19] Two-bit tyrants will force people into compliance with their ever-changing laws. Happiness is the result of setting personal and social behavior in alignment with God's law.

July 26

*How blessed are those who observe His testimonies,
Who seek Him with all their heart.*

PSALM 119:2

Gaining traction" is the effort to get momentum toward a desired goal. The harder it is to dig in, the more intense must be the effort. When we don't seem to "gain traction" in experiencing God, we are tempted to back off. Yet the problem may have been all along that we were half-hearted. God is seeking us with His whole heart, and He wants us to seek Him with the totality of our heart. When we're struggling with His will and plan, it's not time to hesitate or slow down, but to hurl ourselves into seeking Him. That's when we gain traction.

July 27

How blessed is he whose help is the God of Jacob,
Whose hope is in the LORD his God.

PSALM 146:5

It was one of those jarring phone calls a pastor gets sometime. "My daughter's in jail," the distraught mother said. "I want you to go and talk with her!" I asked her to tell me the story. The daughter was twenty-two years old and had been raised in a home with no spiritual background, no concept of Christ. "I've always heard if you train up a child in the way she should go it would turn out alright," the mother said. But the problem is you can't claim a promise unless you've entered God's covenant. Jacob's God becomes *your* hope only when He is your Lord.

July 28

Who may ascend into the hill of the LORD?
And who may stand in His holy place?
He who has clean hands and a pure heart,
He shall receive a blessing from the LORD.

PSALM 24:3-5

Way up there on Zion was the Ark of God, blazing with searing glory, and way down there in the valley stood David with murderous hands and adulterous heart. But the only people qualified to approach God are those with unpolluted outward behavior and pristine motives and thoughts. By such standards, we are unqualified to climb that windy hill. Many believe to get qualified for the climb we must start *doing*. The truth is we must start *being*. When our being is in Christ, His blood penetrates to the deepest, darkest cavern of our soul and purifies it. He has gone behind the veil, and, in Him, we can go too.

July 29

Behold, how good and how pleasant it is
For brothers to dwell together in unity!
It is like the precious oil upon the head,
Coming down upon the beard,
Even Aaron's beard,
Coming down upon the edge of his robes.

PSALM 133:1-2

Family reunions can be happy celebrations. Every year the Huffs—my mother's family—gather in a little metal building outside Laurel, Mississippi, to feast, swap jokes and stories, and marvel over growing-up kids. Jo Beth's kin meets at Blue Mountain College, her *alma mater*, where the focus is fun, fun, fun. God-centered unity among kin—spiritual and physical brothers and sisters—is energizing as it spreads from Jesus Christ, the "head," down the edges of the "robe," the whole community.

July 30

By the blessing of the upright a city is exalted,
But by the mouth of the wicked it is torn down.

PROVERBS 11:11

The upright are up-front. The more such straight-forward individuals make up a population, the more respected and revered the family, city, or nation. A friend was building a fence, and when he got tired of setting his leveling device by each slat, he decided instead to "eyeball" straightness. Twenty-seven slats later he had to tear out the fence and begin again, because the slight margin by which each was off expanded until the whole fence was crooked. Jesus Christ is the standard by which uprightness is set. The more we are aligned by and in Him, the greater blessing we are to all those around us.

July 31

*For there is no distinction between
Jew and Greek; for the same Lord is Lord of all,
abounding in riches for all who call on Him.*

ROMANS 10:12

Years ago, when Lee Beth—our oldest grandchild—visited us, she would head for the "secret drawer," crammed with candy. I can still see the little girl running her fingers through the abundance of delights. God's promise to His children is "abounding riches." We trivialize the promise when we think only of money—or candy. God's abounding riches are never at risk, and they always bear hefty dividends. Many focus on building up riches for retirement but don't consider eternity. The riches of God's covenant are available for all who ask for His salvation in Christ. He wants an open, not a "secret" drawer.

August

*"Whoever then humbles himself as this child,
he is the greatest in the kingdom of heaven."*

MATTHEW 18:4

Three things about a child that could have drawn the Lord's focus: First, children know the limits of the load they can carry. Second, a child understands he or she doesn't understand everything. Third, a little one is willing to rest in the load-bearer and source of answers. Asking questions is one of a child's most notable features. They especially love inquiring, "Why?" But neither are they timid about crying, "Help me, Daddy!" Greatness in the Kingdom of God is recognizing human limitations, coming to the Father for help and understanding, and resting in His arms and answers.

August 2

God has chosen the foolish things of the world to shame the wise, and God has chosen the weak things of the world to shame the things which are strong, and the base things of the world and the despised God has chosen, the things that are not, so that He may nullify the things that are, so that no man may boast before God.

1 CORINTHIANS 1:27-29

Frank Sinatra's "My Way" is one of the most-recorded songs in the history of pop music. It's no surprise. When things seem to be going along "our way" we can continue walking in deception. Only when our foolishness fails do we see what our hearts are really like. Blindness opened Samson's eyes. He saw that he was not a strong man after all, but only a weak man in whom God had demonstrated his mighty power. Our weakness brings us to the highest level of usability in God's Kingdom.

August 3

"And I will bless those who bless you,
And the one who curses you I will curse.
And in you all the families of the earth will be blessed."

GENESIS 12:3

When I was a kid reading the Bible I figured I could skip the genealogies. In some chapters, "begats" abound. The Holy Spirit includes these lists to tell us that the hand of God has been upon His covenant people all along. From the time God revealed His family plan to Abraham, all the way to Jesus Christ—the pinnacle of that family tree— God has been guiding the process. God chose Abraham's family to bless all the families of the earth by being the line through whom the world's Messiah would come. The genealogies show the faithfulness of the God of promise.

August 4

Faithful is He who calls you,
and He also will bring it to pass.

1 THESSALONIANS 5:24

Young men during World War II opened their
mail to find letters announcing they had been
drafted into the armed forces. The assignment was
to defeat the enemy. And when they were called
up to service, the young soldiers were supplied
with resources to carry out the mission. God calls
us to the warfare that rages for control of the
world, supplies us with the implements of battle,
but then does something far greater: He carries
out the mission through us. It is as if President
Roosevelt, the American commander-in-chief
during the Second World War, did the fighting
through the soldiers his government drafted.

August 5

As for God, His way is blameless;
The word of the LORD is tried;
He is a shield to all who take refuge in Him.

PSALM 18:30

It's illogical to blame God, rather than the devil, for the bad things that happen to us. People say that if God is all-powerful, He could have prevented their tragedies. God allows us freedom, and that means accidents can happen. But God's promise is to provide meaning and blessing through the things that happen to His covenant people. A world without God can only look to blind fate and has no hope in the face of suffering. Those who trust in God discover He is blameless and that He shields them from the destructive objectives Satan tries to accomplish through their hurts.

240

August 6

The sacrifices of God are a broken spirit;
A broken and a contrite heart, O God,
You will not despise.

PSALM 51:17

Years ago comedian Red Skelton was on an airplane that developed engine trouble over the Alps. He tried to cheer people with jokes. Finally, the aircraft was nursed to an emergency landing. "Now you can all go back to the sin you turned from a few minutes ago," Skelton reportedly quipped to his fellow passengers.[20] Shallow repentance is really regret, especially over possible consequences. Godly repentance is, as they say in the military, an "about face," a turn away from sin to God. It comes when our hearts are broken over our sin rather than merely anxious about the outcome.

August 7

For as in Adam all die,
so also in Christ all will be made alive.

1 CORINTHIANS 15:22

We share the destiny of the vessel we inhabit. An Egyptian pilot committed suicide after take-off from New York by crashing his airplane. All aboard perished with him. The sentence of eternal separation from God is on Adam. Every human being born is automatically "in Adam," because he is the first biological parent. We all go down in flames with Adam unless we can be transferred to another vessel. That's what God does in Jesus Christ. Adam was the rebel, Jesus the obedient Son. He reverses the curse Adam brought on himself and his race. Jesus brings us into the new race, destined for blessing.

August 8

*The Lord knows how to rescue
the godly from temptation.*

2 PETER 2:9

The little girl pled with her brother and sister to jump from the second floor of their burning home. "Fear kept the youngsters from following her and cost them their lives," a newspaper reported.[21] If we're caught in the conflagration of temptation, perhaps we've refused rescue. The children in the burning house were afraid to leap, but sometimes we reject God's rescue because we're reluctant to give up pleasures the temptation offers. There was no need for the children to perish in the fire, and there is never a need for God's covenant people to be trapped in temptation, because His rescue is always available.

August 9

For His anger is but for a moment,
His favor is for a lifetime;
Weeping may last for the night,
But a shout of joy comes in the morning.

PSALM 30:5

There was evening and there was morning," says Genesis, chapter 1, and so the sequence has been for eons. There is an evening of our lives as well as a day announced by sparkling mornings. In the dark nights, vision is overwhelmed with sorrow and crisis, but the sunshine of the morning drives away the haunting torments of the night, and there is the shout of joy. God's promise to His covenant people is that morning will always follow night. And the time will come when night no longer drags morning into its dark pit. The great eternal morning will prevail, and the joy-shouting will be the music of the spheres.

244

The mouth of the righteous flows with wisdom.

PROVERBS 10:31

Dr. F. B. Thorn, a former pastor of our church, carried his Bible in a paper sack, but a prankster once replaced the Bible with a catalog. Dr. Thorn reached into the sack for his Bible. His friend, the practical joker, could hardly contain his laughter when Dr. Thorn's hand hit the catalog instead. But Dr. Thorn had the last laugh. He had committed Scripture to memory, and he preached on verses he quoted by heart. In fact, the sermon was so powerful, almost everyone was shouting "Amen!" at every profound point. The mouth of the righteous does indeed flow with the wisdom of God.

August 11

*"But the word is very near you, in your mouth
and in your heart, that you may observe it."*

DEUTERONOMY 30:14

A catalyst precipitates change. The Word of God came into unformed nothing and was catalytic, creating the universe. God's Word sets up transformation in whatever it enters. The same creative Word that sparked worlds is implanted in the hearts of human beings. God gives us capacity to draw up that Word through speech. It can have a catalytic work in our lives as we observe and put it into practice, and the catalytic Word can transform others as we speak it to them.

*Augu**st** 12*

*But what does it say? "THE WORD IS NEAR YOU,
IN YOUR MOUTH AND IN YOUR HEART"—
that is, the word of faith which we are preaching,
that if you confess with your mouth Jesus as Lord,
and believe in your heart that God raised Him
from the dead, you will be saved.*

ROMANS 10:8-9

The God-embedded catalytic Word is that of
faith. The world is full of law religions, from
Judaism and Islam to secular systems of political
correctness. Rituals, feasts, attendance at synagogue,
mosque, temple, or cathedral, following the eight
steps of Buddhism or the five prayers of the Muslim,
or washing in the Ganges, all are characteristics of
law religion. But a Hebrew scholar named Paul
declares it's all wrong. Salvation is resting one's
eternal destiny in the One to whom all the Jewish
rituals pointed—Jesus Christ.

August 13

He has also set eternity in their heart.

ECCLESIASTES 3:11

A famous explorer was recounting his adventures to a swarm of reporters. "Sir," one asked, "do you plan ever to explore any unknown areas?" The explorer replied, "Yes, I plan to make one last expedition. Only one Man has been to this place and come back alive. He promised He will take me there and let me explore it." A reporter fired back, "Are you saying you believe in Heaven?" "Absolutely," replied the explorer. "There has to be a Heaven, because it as been implanted in the hearts of all people throughout history."

August 14

"When you pass through the waters, I will be with you;
And through the rivers, they will not overflow you.
When you walk through the fire, you will not be scorched,
Nor will the flame burn you."

ISAIAH 43:2

Israel lost its song in Babylon. Our Babylon is the fallen world system. Sometimes it robs us of our song. But we get the music back when we remember God. The waters are symbols of separation from all you love, and the rivers seemingly impassable boundaries between you and everything you care about. The fire is the looming danger that can turn your hopes to ashes. But God's promise to His covenant people is that there is no ocean He can't split, no rivers He can't cut a path through, and no fire He can't quench. That'll put the music back in your heart.

August 15

The Lord GOD is my strength,
And He has made my feet like hinds' feet,
And makes me walk on my high places.

HABAKKUK 3:19

A rookie cowboy was assigned to take cattle to high pasture. "You can't go up there," said an old cowpoke, pointing to a high ridge. "I can ride as well as anybody," said the novice. "But the problem is your horse," the experienced cowhand replied. He then explained that to ride the ridge, a horse had to track like deer. Rather than flaying out, the back feet had to fall in the exact tracks as the front feet. When our feet track with God's, when we walk where He walks, we find strength.

August 16

So the ransomed of the LORD will return
And come with joyful shouting to Zion,
And everlasting joy will be on their heads.
They will obtain gladness and joy,
And sorrow and sighing will flee away.

ISAIAH 51:11

You and I are in a big race. There are two tracks.
We can run the Sinai Marathon, or we can
dash on the Zion Course. Both marathons have
their own sounds. The Sinai run is full of wheezes
and "O me!" utterances. The Zion Marathon is
punctuated with shouts of joy. Sinai is the
performance track. This smoky mountain is wreathed
in mystery and otherness. The Zion run is the grace
race. Those on the Sinai course don't know if they'll
win the prize or not. Those running the Zion route
are speeding toward the prize they've already won.
No wonder they "come with joyful shouting to Zion."

August 17

Be anxious for nothing, but in everything by prayer and supplication with thanksgiving let your requests be made known to God. And the peace of God, which surpasses all comprehension, will guard your hearts and your minds in Christ Jesus.

PHILIPPIANS 4:6-7

Prayer is to worry what an antibiotic is to nagging infection. It's not religious, rote ceremonial prayer, but worshipful prayer. Such communion with God recognizes His all-encompassing power and authority right up front. Worry-zapping prayer is also supplication, which is praying passionately like Jesus in Gethsemane. The prayer that overwhelms worry is also thanksgiving. As you are grateful for past blessings, you gain assurance for the future. If you're God's covenant child through Christ, you don't have to drink your anxieties away, but pray them away.

252

August 18

Delight yourself in the LORD;
And He will give you the desires of your heart.

PSALM 37:4

Distorted teaching says if you've ever wanted health and wealth, if you delight yourself in the Lord, He will give them to you. But if you truly delight in the Lord, you will want what He wants: the advance of His Kingdom in the world. Accomplishing that mission will become your heart's desire. If health and wealth will get it done, health and wealth you may have. But if a rugged, bloody cross is His means for you, one will be spiked in the ground just ahead of you. But you will run toward it like Jesus, "who, for the joy set before Him, endured the cross" (Hebrews 12:2).

August 19

"Ho! Every one who thirsts, come to the waters;
And you who have no money come, buy and eat.
Come, buy wine and milk
Without money and without cost."

ISAIAH 55:1

Thirst comes from dryness, the lack of fluid, and lack is need. So hunger is the result of missing food. Popular culture does all possible to disguise its spiritual thirsting and hunger. A man noted his associate cramming in breath mints and concluded he must have had garlic for lunch. "Nope," the friend replied, "in fact I missed lunch, and these mints fool my stomach into thinking it's had real food." If we're going to luxuriate in God's waters and feast on His spread, we need to quit swallowing breath mints, acknowledge our true thirst and hunger, and we will be filled to overflowing.

*"For if you forgive others for their transgressions,
your heavenly Father will also forgive you.
But if you do not forgive others, then your
Father will not forgive your transgressions."*

MATTHEW 6:14-15

During South Africa's apartheid regime, a certain man was imprisoned on Robben Island, just off Cape Town, where Nelson Mandela was held. Nightly, a cruel guard beat the prisoner. When the apartheid government was replaced with one led by Mandela himself, he urged forgiveness. One day the man who had shared his prison suddenly encountered the guard who had beaten him. The former security man tensed, believing he would be attacked. Instead, the ex-prisoner embraced him and told him he forgave him. The promise of God is that we are forgiven in proportion to forgiving those who've hurt us.

*I know that the LORD will
maintain the cause of the afflicted.*

PSALM 140:12

The "afflicted" are those overwhelmed by circumstances. The weight of anguish threatens to drag them down into depression's murky depths. God's promise to His covenant people drifting in a sea of despair is that He will keep them afloat. Opponents add lead to the strain of disappointment, and the suction grows. But God's sustaining strength increases proportionately, and it's always mightier than the pull downward.

August 22

Then I saw a new heaven and a new earth;
for the first heaven and the first earth passed away,
and there is no longer any sea.

REVELATION 21:1

Ultimately all our grief is tied to loss and separation. Your heart may be broken because death has taken someone special from you. Or, your loss may have been in reputation. Maybe your character got caught in a vise of lies, and people who were once your friends are now your enemies. Perhaps what you've lost is a job and financial security. Loss is the heart of heartbreak. God's coming Kingdom has no separating ocean. There are no sails fading on the horizon, bearing loved ones away from us. In His Kingdom, there is no loss.

August 23

Cast your bread on the surface of the waters,
for you will find it after many days.

ECCLESIASTES 11:1

Solomon dispatched his ships to the exotic places of his day. Sometimes they would sail as far as India. The trading vessels would be gone perhaps four years, but the day would come when their billowing sheets would be visible again on the horizon, bearing precious treasures. The generous heart is an investing heart. It expects no return, yet in extending its kindness, kindness is its return—with interest. It may take years to see the blessing flow back, but it does inevitably.

August 24

Your word I have treasured in my heart,
That I may not sin against You.

PSALM 119:11

There are nine filters through which decisions and actions should be run, executive coach Brad Hays tells leaders.[22] The first is God Himself, and the second is God's Word. If the action doesn't glorify God and line up with what Jesus would do, it should be screened out. If there is no biblical support for the intended behavior, then it should be eliminated. That requires that a man or woman have God's Word stored up inside and treasured as the most valuable standard for decisions and behaviors.

August 25

For sin shall not be master over you,
for you are not under law but under grace.

ROMANS 6:14

President Lincoln understood the ruin slavery was bringing to individuals, families, and the nation, and, in 1863, he issued the Emancipation Proclamation, freeing the slaves. But it took a long time for the declaration of liberty to reach the scattered plantations and slave quarters. Even when I was a child in the Deep South, signs marked facilities for "White" and "Colored." Let the word go out that the old slave master of sin has been defeated by Jesus Christ. Humanity's Emancipation Proclamation has been signed with His blood.

August 26

If we confess our sins, He is faithful and
righteous to forgive us our sins and to cleanse us
from all unrighteousness.

1 JOHN 1:9

Without the concept of sin there is no understanding of forgiveness. Without forgiveness, there is no resolution of our deepest needs and anxieties. God doesn't call us to confess our sins because He wants us rolling in guilt, but because until we acknowledge the problem we can't be cured. Denial is imprisoning. But when there is honest confrontation with our personal sins, there is the release of forgiveness and grace from God, Who alone is holy and has the authority to put away our guilt.

'Call to Me and I will answer you, and I will tell you great and mighty things, which you do not know.'

JEREMIAH 33:3

Caller ID is a blessing and curse. We can avoid talking to phoners we want to avoid, but we sometimes miss important conversations. Perhaps you've made a call and suspected the other person saw your name and number but simply wasn't ready to talk. You waited for a response. Caller ID isn't a means of avoiding calls for God. He looks eagerly at who is calling on Him, and He always takes the call. So often today we get a computer rather than a human voice, and we yearn to hear a live person. When we call on God we always get Him, and He always answers.

August 28

For this is contained in Scripture:
"BEHOLD, I LAY IN ZION A CHOICE STONE,
A PRECIOUS CORNER STONE, AND HE WHO
BELIEVES IN HIM WILL NOT BE DISAPPOINTED."

1 PETER 2:6

In building the Texas capitol, only one type of stone would do—pink marble quarried from Granite Mountain near Marble Falls, Texas. "Texas Pink" was the choice stone for the building that stands in Austin. There's plenty of other stone in Texas, but it wasn't deemed worthy for the capitol. There's an abundance of material for the foundation and structure of a human life, but there's only one "choice stone"—the Lord Jesus Christ. All else is pebbles or crumbling shale.

August 29

"When you pass through the waters, I will be with you;
And through the rivers, they will not overflow you.
When you walk through the fire, you will not be scorched,
Nor will the flame burn you."

ISAIAH 43:2

Architects of the current Texas capitol chose marble because the previous structure burned in 1881. In 1888, the new home of Texas government was dedicated, and it stands today. Fires rage in the fallen world, and sometimes God's people have to walk through them. We will pass through "many tribulations" (Acts 14:22), but those whose lives are built on, in, and through Jesus will not be burned up, any more than a building constructed of granite or marble. They will be like Shadrach, Meshach, and Abednego, who found in Babylon's searing furnace the very presence of God.

August 30

For those whom He foreknew, He also predestined to become conformed to the image of His Son, so that He would be the firstborn among many brethren.

ROMANS 8:29

When I was a boy our small community didn't qualify for a Ringling Brothers performance, but a smaller circus visited us annually. I remember especially a toothless, defanged bear dancing at the end of a chain. Decades later I remember how "unbearish" he looked. We're like the poor animal. Sin diminished God's image in us. The promise of God is that we are going to be brought back into the fullness of our being, which is conformity to Jesus Christ. We will no longer be less than what God designed humans to be, because we will be conformed to all Jesus is.

*And we desire that each one of you show
the same diligence so as to realize the full assurance
of hope until the end, so that you will not be
sluggish, but imitators of those who through
faith and patience inherit the promises.*

HEBREWS 6:11-12

Claiming God's promises is not like cashing in a lottery ticket. Faith and patience are required. There are four elements to consider. First, "understand." Sometimes we attempt to claim promises out of context. Understanding the biblical background is vital. Second, "ask." Is the promise limited or unlimited, conditional or unconditional? Is the Holy Spirit leading me to claim the particular promise? Third, claim the promise. The previous steps require patience, and claiming requires faith. Finally, "act" on the promise. Begin setting behavior and plans, based on the promise you have claimed through Christ.

September

September 1

The name of the LORD is a strong tower;
The righteous runs into it and is safe.

PROVERBS 18:10

All people know titles for God—the "Great Spirit," "Ground of All Being," "the Man Upstairs"—but only those in covenant know His name. Each biblical name of God reflects some blessing or favor available to those who know His name. "The Lord Is My Peace," The Lord Is My Righteousness," "The Lord Is My Healer," and "The Lord Is My Provider" all reveal what God is in interaction and engagement with people. Together, the names of God revealed in the Bible are the stones comprising the "strong tower." No wonder His people are safe and secure when we run into it for sanctuary.

*Then Gideon built an altar there to the LORD
and named it The LORD is Peace.*

JUDGES 6:24

The Lord is our peace. Not family, not possessions. Not world conditions or the political situation. God's covenant children need not be dependent— or co-pendent—on anyone or anything for their peace. In fact, when personal peace depends on anything but God, it's fragile as a spider's web. The person in Christ is not cold or indifferent; rather, the suffering of others, broken relationships, and world troubles stir compassion, prayer, and godly deeds. But the people trusting in Christ place ultimate reliance for the outworking of all things upon God. And they say, "The Lord is my peace."

Moses built an altar and named it
The LORD is My Banner.

EXODUS 17:15

When the enemy thunders down on the Hebrews in the wilderness, Moses lifts up his staff and calls down the power of God. The rod wasn't magic, but it symbolized that the Jews were marching under the banner of the true God. It was as if Moses' staff had a flag attached. It symbolized the source of their aid, their allegiance, and their alignment. When the Lord is our banner, we declare that our aid comes from Him, our allegiance is to Him and His Kingdom, and we align with His values and character as our standard.

> *Abraham called the name of that place*
> *The LORD Will Provide, as it is said to this day, "In the*
> *mount of the LORD it will be provided."*

GENESIS 22:14

Just as Abraham was about to plunge the sacrificial knife into Isaac's heart, he heard the ram bleating in the bush. Why does God seem to wait until the last minute to bring our provision? The reality is we must be empty before we will receive His fullness. It wasn't Isaac who had to die that day, but Abraham—to his own possessions, plans, prospects and perspectives. Most of us have to go to extremes to get to that point; hence, God's seeming "last minute" provision. But when we receive the fullness of His provision, all we've given up seems shabby.

September 5

"I, the LORD, am your healer."

EXODUS 15:26

God's covenant people have the promise of a new body in eternity, free of disease, alive with the quality of Christ's resurrection body. When Adam sinned, death moved from spirit to soul to body. Salvation flows the same way. God heals people in the fallen world by direct and indirect means, using both supernatural and natural methods, including medical science, which is part of His general revelation. For His covenant people, healing is a certainty, and the only questions are: When will it be manifest? How will it be achieved? Where—in earth or Heaven? Healing is in God's covenant, and all health comes from Him.

September 6

*"You shall not worship any other god, for the LORD,
whose name is Jealous, is a jealous God."*

EXODUS 34:14

Covetousness and envy are wrong, but appropriate
jealousy is a dimension of passionate love. To be
jealous of a business rival or of someone considered
more attractive is actually to covet, and therefore a
violation of God's commandment. But if a third
party intervenes in a marriage, the offended
individual will be rightly jealous if love is present.
Jealousy allows for no rivals in intimate relationships.
This is why God is jealous when His people embrace
idolatry. Be grateful He is jealous for you, because
it's a sign of the intensity of His love for you.

September 7

*"This is His name by which He will be called,
'The LORD our righteousness.'"*

JEREMIAH 23:6

To be righteous is to align with God's holy character in every facet of one's being. This is the requirement for being in relationship with God in this world and for gaining entry into Heaven. A while back, billionaire Warren Buffet transferred a huge chunk of his wealth to a charity started by billionaire Bill Gates. But in God's economy, He transfers the immeasurable wealth of His righteousness to your account through Jesus Christ. Before Christ, you and I kept coming up short of God's glory—His holiness. Now the treasure of His holiness is ours.

"'I am the LORD who sanctifies you.'"

EXODUS 31:13

Sanctification is setting apart something or someone for the exclusive use of something else. The bride and groom vow that they are "forsaking all others." Being sanctified by and for God is the commitment of your whole being for Him alone. Sanctification is to be made holy, and is both an event and a process. The moment you receive Christ, you are holy in God's sight, because you have the righteousness of His spotless Son. But the process of sanctification happens in the material world as you progressively place more and more of yourself under His complete control. This leads to practical living consistent with your heavenly character.

Blessed be the LORD, my rock.

PSALM 144:1

God's covenant names are revealed as people engage with Him in the turbulent world. We know Him best in the intense interactions arising from lives under constant duress. Pounding waves of threat, fear and danger run at us, but He is like the great stone outcroppings along the California and Oregon coasts. We best understand and appreciate Him as "rock" when oceans of trial mount toward us. The tides shatter when they collide with the rock. If we are in Him, the tsunamis that would sweep us away are reduced to splinters of white foam instead.

> The name of the city from that day shall be,
> 'The LORD is there.'"

EZEKIEL 48:35

Ezekiel's theme is "The Lord is there." The prophet's immediate audience was Jews in Babylonian exile. The Temple symbolizing God's nearness was in Jerusalem far away. Babylon seemed remote from God. But the Holy Spirit's message to people in exile—then and now—is that they are not removed from God's presence. Ezekiel himself experienced God's presence in visions. He became a reporter. God's call on His people today is to report to all sharing the land of exile with them that they have met God in this strange place, and that He is as much God in Babylon as in Jerusalem.

The LORD is His name.

EXODUS 15:3

To call God *Adonai*—Lord—is to acknowledge that someone is in control, and that it is Him. Some nonbelievers see history as careening through time, like a car without a driver. "History," said Henry Ford, "is more or less bunk."[23] Karl Marx and his followers believed history to be under the control of economic dynamics. But the name *Adonai* means that history is neither hapless chance nor controlled by impersonal forces. The throne of the universe is occupied by the One whose name is Lord.

Then David said to the Philistine, "You come to me with a sword, a spear, and a javelin, but I come to you in the name of the LORD of hosts."

1 SAMUEL 17:45

Nations with immense nuclear capabilities must practice restraint, but many press their governments to crush every skirmish with an atom-capped missile. The Lord of hosts could have unleashed twelve legions of angels to rescue Jesus from the cross, but He allowed the carnage because the world's salvation depended on the completion of the atonement mission. We live in the tension of knowing that God is Lord of hosts, while apparent disaster takes shape around us. We cry for the blasts of the angelic hosts, but we finally rest in knowing He has defended us from much worse than what our limited vision can see.

Then she called the name of the LORD who spoke to her,
"You are a God who sees."

GENESIS 16:13

Hagar was an outcast servant girl, pregnant by her master, Abram. Out in the desert, Abram no longer watches over her, but the desperate slave encounters the One whose eyes count. She is no theologian, so she calls God by the way she understands Him—*El Roi*. Her encounter with God-Who-Sees teaches us much. When we are in desperate solitude—as was Hagar—His eyes are on us. God lays out the future of Hagar's descendants, showing that God-Who-Sees-Us enables us to see. He sees all His creation, but *El Roi* has a special eye for His covenant children.

Then Moses said to God, "Behold, I am going to the sons of Israel, and I will say to them, 'The God of your fathers has sent me to you.' Now they may say to me, 'What is His name?' What shall I say to them?" God said to Moses, "I AM WHO I AM"; and He said, "Thus you shall say to the sons of Israel, 'I AM has sent me to you.'"

EXODUS 3:13–14

God's being is eternally present tense. Tribal and national gods—like those of Pharaoh's Egypt—would come and go. But Moses went in the authority of the everlasting God. That He is I-Am-That-I-Am means He is back there in your past, reforming its wreckage into a beautiful testimony. He's in your future, preparing places, people, and events by which He will work good into your life and advance His Kingdom for you. I-Am-That-I-Am is engaged with you in the here and now, but He is also sublimely above it.

"She will bear a Son; and you shall call His name Jesus,
for He will save His people from their sins."
Now all this took place to fulfill what was spoken by
the Lord through the prophet: . . .
"AND THEY SHALL CALL HIS NAME IMMANUEL,"
which translated means, "GOD WITH US."

MATTHEW 1:21-23

The mounting up of God's names leads to the peak—Jesus, Immanuel, the Christ. Through His names, God was saying things about His nature and character as revealed through people living in time and space. All the other names were fragmentary views, each showing some facet of God. Jesus reveals the totality of God. The Old Testament people saw God as through a prism, but we have the joy of seeing His fullness. As Jesus is the ultimate name of God, so Jesus is the ultimate promise of God. Know Him and you know God.

*But know that the LORD has
set apart the godly man for Himself.*

PSALM 4:3

A Houston woman acquired a chair once owned by France's King Louis XIV. Visitors to her mansion could look at the antique, but a velvet rope across it forbad anyone sitting in the chair. It was set apart from the other furniture, priceless and precious. God places certain things under the "ban." They are His alone. He shares the bounty of creation with us, but when He marks something for Himself, it is His exclusively. What an honor to be set apart for God. Those men and women who've entered covenant with Christ have His identifying mark on them, and they belong to Him and no one else.

They will not hurt or destroy
in all My holy mountain,
For the earth will be full of the knowledge
of the LORD
As the waters cover the sea.

ISAIAH 11:9

In physics, "displacement" means a dense object pushes aside the less heavy. So a ship displaces water, allowing the vessel to float. The knowledge of God is a displacing force. Wherever His truth and righteous enter, deceit and evil are pushed aside. God promises a day will come when the knowledge of Him will fill the earth so totally that all evil and its lies will be forced out of the world completely. Hell is the sewer where all sin goes. In that day, there will no longer be adversarial relationships, and animals and humans alike will dwell in security.

"My people will be satisfied with My goodness,"
declares the LORD.

JEREMIAH 31:14

A friend visited the home of the president of a
Central American country. The political leader
collected ancient Indian art. Six-foot stone spheres,
carved by Aztecs, rested in his garden. My friend
marveled at the perfect roundness. There was
something satisfying to his soul about the serene
spheres. Humans have a passion for completeness
ranging from a resolution of disagreements to the
completion of a musical chord. This tendency
points to the deeper need for spiritual satisfaction.
The human psyche cannot rest until that need is
met. The human spirit yearns for God's goodness,
and He promises to satisfy us with it.

September 19

"If I go and prepare a place for you,
I will come again and receive you to Myself,
that where I am, there you may be also."

JOHN 14:3

I once worked in a tunnel, back in the days I thought I would be an engineer. We were boring through an Alabama mountain where a big water conduit was to be placed. One contractor bored from the east, while we dug westward. "Have they broken through yet?" I asked one morning. "Yes," a worker replied. "They broke through last night on the graveyard shift." Years later it hit me: Jesus worked the "graveyard shift" at the cross. He broke through the dark tunnel of death, and when it comes our time, He will come back to us and lead us through.

*"Truly, truly, I say to you, he who believes in Me,
the works that I do, he will do also; and greater works
than these he will do; because I go to the Father."*

JOHN 14:12

The greatness of Jesus' strategy is that He began a global transformation movement with twelve ragtag men in a forgotten nation under occupation by a cruel empire. He stilled storms and fed thousands with fragments of food. He healed the blind, deaf, mute, and lame. Jesus walked on water and burst from the tomb. How can any of us do "greater works" than that? The clue to the promise is in His strategy. Jesus discipled the twelve, but He has empowered His modern disciples to reach and teach the millions.

"WHOEVER WILL CALL ON THE NAME OF THE LORD WILL BE SAVED."

ROMANS 10:13

The brutish Romans forced people to declare, "Caesar is lord!" Those who refused often perished. To call on Christ's name for salvation rather than Caesar's could be costly for Paul's immediate audience. Today we're tempted to think too casually about the implications of Christ's name. Yet there is an empire of darkness that wants our allegiance. Calling on the name of the Lord is declaring that our hearts belong to the Kingdom of God. When we salute the banner of His name by confessing Christ's Lordship, we are saved from the cruel empire of death.

For He will give His angels charge concerning you,
To guard you in all your ways.

PSALM 91:11

When the President of the United States moves from place to place—even a stroll across the White House lawn—He is encircled by a security team. God's covenant people are on mission in the world. As they move about on Kingdom business, God's servants are surrounded by their own squadron. God's angels are His messengers and warriors. Nothing can touch a person on Kingdom business. Some are called to die as martyrs. When that happens, it's not that the angels failed, but that the plan of God succeeded and the individual's mission was completed.

September 23

Return to the LORD your God,
For He is gracious and compassionate,
Slow to anger, abounding in lovingkindness
And relenting of evil.

JOEL 2:13

Imagine four teenage boys in a fishing boat on the Niagara River, tied to a rope. God holds the rope, restraining the boys in safety. Finally they get into some pretty fast water, and God begins to pull back. The adolescents want more thrill and demand He drop the rope. God promised the boys they could be free. With sadness, He lets go of the rope, and gives them over to their dangerous choice. The slowness of God's anger means He is reluctant to turn people loose, but ultimately His faithfulness to His promise of soul-freedom mandates He drop the rope when we continue in rebellion.

September 24

"So you shall keep His statutes and His commandments which I am giving you today, that it may go well with you and with your children after you, and that you may live long on the land which the LORD your God is giving you for all time."

DEUTERONOMY 4:40

"Quality of life" is a key phrase in the twenty-first century. For politicians, "quality of life" means the general welfare of their constituents. God is concerned not only for the personal well-being of His covenant people, but for society in general. Wherever His values and worldview prevail—even among nonbelievers—the culture is blessed with "quality of life." Blessings flow where God's laws are foundational. "Quality of life" is also the blessing of a family or even a business that honors God's ways. Prosperity, liberty, and human dignity all accompany God's "statutes and commandments."

September 25

*"Give, and it will be given to you. They will pour
into your lap a good measure—pressed down,
shaken together, and running over. For by your standard
of measure it will be measured to you in return."*

LUKE 6:38

Most merchandisers believe the secret to sales is in the packaging. Take, for example, breakfast cereal. Some boxes look big enough to feed a football team, but when you open them, there's emptiness at the top. When God pours out His blessings on His covenant people, there's no room for any more. He presses down on the contents so He can add more, shakes the box of blessing one more time, and drops in more, until the container is running over. The key to such bounty is in the desire to receive to bless others, not to hoard for oneself.

September 26

The Lord is not slow about His promise, as some count slowness, but is patient toward you, not wishing for any to perish but for all to come to repentance.

2 PETER 3:9

Often we try to trap God in our time schemes. We lay out plans and schedules and expect Him to conform. God sent His Son into the world as quickly as the world was prepared to receive Him. When the Father saw that the sacrificial system with its types and shadows had been established, and that the prophetic word pointing to the Messiah had been heard, the world was in readiness for the Messiah, and at the precise moment in accord with His plan, sent Him to us—in "the fullness of time" (Galatians 4:4).

*"I will make an everlasting covenant with them
that I will not turn away from them, to do them good;
and I will put the fear of Me in their hearts
so that they will not turn away from Me."*

JEREMIAH 32:40

People are qualified for liberty in proportion to their willingness to place chains on their own hearts, said Edmund Burke. A person without God's fear—or reverence—in his heart requires external restraint. People with internal controls are truly free. When choices come to disobey and rebel or turn toward God, they can be counted on to walk the Lord's way. He doesn't turn away from His covenant people, and God wires them so they won't turn away from Him.

"For the vision is yet for the appointed time;
It hastens toward the goal and it will not fail.
Though it tarries, wait for it;
For it will certainly come, it will not delay."

HABAKKUK 2:3

God's plan unfolds like a Chinese fan. An artist paints a delicate scene of a waterfall, full of color. But the whole fan must be opened before the picture is revealed, and it's opened one panel at a time. Sometimes a section is blank, or nothing but squiggly lines. Periods in our lives make no sense or seem dull. But no panel can be opened before the one preceding it. And it takes all the sections to make up the picture. God is slowly opening His vision for your life and the world, and He knows the appointed time for revealing the parts as well as the whole.

"Behold, as for the proud one,
His soul is not right within him;
But the righteous will live by his faith."

HABAKKUK 2:4

The person trusting God knows three things about God's will. First, God has a plan for his or her life. Second, the individual in covenant with God understands that God is revealing His will, piece by piece, in His own timing. Third, covenant people trust God to bring the whole into being. Faith is resting one's destiny on the Lord. Covenant people live in the balance between passivity and impulsiveness. They wait on the Lord to reveal each step, but they move forward with action, trusting that God is bringing them to His complete purpose for their lives.

For God has not given us a spirit of timidity,
but of power and love and discipline.

2 TIMOTHY 1:7

A common assumption is that leaders are extroverted dynamos who rush through like tornadoes. The Bible gives a different picture. Timothy seems to have been an introvert, yet Paul counted on him many times to carry out vital leadership tasks. Leadership is qualitative— wisdom, knowledge, faith, courage. The personality package will vary, introverted as well as extroverted. God will give boldness even to His shy covenant people. He will endow the seeming milk-toast personality with surprising authority, the apparently cold with burning love, and the butterfly-type with amazing discipline.

October

October 1

The joy of the LORD is your strength. . . .
Sing for joy to God our strength.

NEHEMIAH 8:10; PSALM 81:1

I grew up in the comic book era. There were no cartoons on TV. In fact, there was no TV in the average home. But the comic books brought us Captain Marvel, Superman, and many more characters all in lavish color. Almost all the comic books carried the same ad. A skinny fellow lay on a beach while a bully kicked sand at him. A year later, the runt has completed the "Charles Atlas" course, and flattens the bully. Satan bullies us constantly, humiliating and harassing us. But in God's joy, we rise up in new strength and put the bully to flight.

October 2

You have taught children and nursing infants to give you praise. They silence your enemies who were seeking revenge.

PSALM 8:2 NLT

My childhood home was in a small town but sandwiched close to other houses. The next door neighbor had twenty-six dogs. At night they would howl like packs of banshees. During World War II, my dad worked two shifts and needed sleep. One night he could stand the howling no longer, and went out to our car and laid down on the horn. He told the neighbor he would stop the blare when the dogs ceased their barking. When God's people lift up the joyful noise of praise and worship, the powers of darkness are silenced. Praising God mutes the enemy.

October 3

It is more blessed to give than to receive.

ACTS 20:35

A man visited a church each Sunday for a month or so during the annual stewardship campaign. He listened to tithing testimonies and appeals for pledges and contributions. "All I've heard in this church is 'giving, giving, giving,'" he wrote the pastor. "Thank you for your note," the pastor replied. "You have given me the most practical definition of Christianity I ever heard. This is exactly what a real Christian is—giving, giving, giving." God gave us His Son, who gave us His life. To be in the image of God is to be a giver.

October 4

"In those days they will not say again,
'The fathers have eaten sour grapes,
And the children's teeth are set on edge.'
But everyone will die for his own iniquity; each man
who eats the sour grapes, his teeth will be set on edge."

JEREMIAH 31:29-30

Family legends suggest my forebears were Alabama bootleggers. It bothered me as a child that I would pay for their sins. Under the New Covenant, made in Jesus Christ, we become responsible for our own sin—not the sins of our ancestors. Were it not for Christ we would stand in eternity guilty of the sins of our parentage, all the way back to Adam. But in Christ, we become new creations with a new family—that of God. There's no sin heritage in that family tree, and nothing for which we must give account except our own sin. And all our iniquity has been removed by Christ's blood.

October 5

"While the earth remains,
Seedtime and harvest,
And cold and heat,
And summer and winter,
And day and night shall not cease."

GENESIS 8:22

McGuffey's Reader told of a man who collided with one of God's moral laws. Angrily, he said, "I wish I lived in a world of chance!" The next morning he wanted to soothe a toothache with warm coffee. As he sipped, the coffee turned to ice. He yelled, "What's the meaning of this?" A voice replied, "You now live in a world of chance. Sometimes you boil water and it might be hot, and at other times it might freeze." God's promise to humanity through Noah is that we will not occupy a world where the foundational order is destroyed. He will not abandon us to raw chance.

October 6

Your toil is not in vain in the Lord.

1 CORINTHIANS 15:58

Outside the covenants of promise, people see themselves abandoned to Fate or meaninglessness. But God's promise to those who trust Him is that there is nothing vain, empty, or meaningless that is done in, for, and through Him. Those outside Christ may see no redeeming value in suffering, no purpose. Tears and blood lead nowhere but to more anguish. God's covenant is that every tear has meaning, every drop of blood leads to new life. Nothing is empty and meaningless in His Kingdom.

October 7

"Take My yoke upon you and learn from Me,
for I am gentle and humble in heart,
and YOU WILL FIND REST FOR YOUR SOULS.
For My yoke is easy and My burden is light."

MATTHEW 11:29-30

Many years ago, I was preaching on Christ's yoke. "I wish I had a yoke," I said one Sunday. A farmer rummaged an old yoke from behind his barn and brought it down the aisle the next week, completely surprising me. I discovered yokes are thick and heavy, and the secret to getting cattle into a yoke is the fit. If a yoke wears well, the oxen don't resist it, and it enables them to stay together, on track. Jesus promises that His yoke is just right for each of us. When we're under the yoke of His Lordship, we rest, knowing we are guided by the Master.

October 8

Train up a child in the way he should go,
Even when he is old he will not depart from it.

PROVERBS 22:6

Construction crews don't wait until the building is half finished to lay the foundation. Training a child means building into his or her life early the solid base of a biblical worldview. It's also is to let them see in you a life that stands on unshakable foundations. "Where did I go wrong?" some parents ask—even among the churchgoing. Perhaps the children saw little or no evidence of God's truth, consistency with the parents' confession, or practical application of biblical values. Lay the foundation, show them what a life under Christ's Lordship looks like, and you will experience the promise.

October 9

"And they overcame him because of the blood of the Lamb and because of the word of their testimony, and they did not love their life even when faced with death."

REVELATION 12:11

As a boy, I was a soprano. A teacher even tried to get me on the radio. Then my voice changed, and with it my life—at least that part of it. God promises to build a testimony in His people. Interacting with challenges, engaging with people, and experiencing life's tensions as a committed follower of Christ all build the testimony of His faithfulness. Your "voice" will "change," and what you once regarded as magnificent will be seen as the five-watt radio station it really was. Your new voice—your testimony—will lead to overcoming strength, which will be broadcast loudly and clearly to others.

October 10

For Your name's sake You will lead me and guide me.

PSALM 31:3

One of our sons had difficulty riding a bicycle. A buddy learned to ride before he did, so my boy wanted to jump on and catch up with his friend. I worked with him, holding the seat, helping him keep balance, scooting him along. There were minor calamities, with scratches and tears, but I wouldn't leave his side. As we ride through life, sometimes tottering and uncertain, our heavenly Father holds on, picks us up when we fall, cleans us up, forgives us, and sets us rolling again. Just because we fall doesn't mean He leaves our side.

October 11

"But love your enemies, and do good, and lend, expecting nothing in return; and your reward will be great, and you will be sons of the Most High; for He Himself is kind to ungrateful and evil men."

LUKE 6:35

Helen Thomas, long-time White House correspondent, became noted for her stinging sarcasm. Late in her career, she said, "I censored myself for fifty years when I was a reporter. Now I wake up and ask myself, who do I hate today?"[24] Jesus tells His followers to scan the horizon daily and see who needs His love—even among a person's enemies. Thomas received notoriety, but Jesus' people practicing His love will get the only applause that matters, that from the Most High.

Against You, You only, I have sinned
And done what is evil in Your sight,
So that You are justified when You speak
And blameless when You judge....
Purify me with hyssop, and I shall be clean;
Wash me, and I shall be whiter than snow.

PSALM 51:4, 7

For years, a certain golden eagle patrolled a point off the Hawaiian island, Maui. The big creature was a spectacular sight hovering over the junction of land and sea. One day a helicopter strayed into its territory. The eagle attacked, and all that was found was one feather. Sinful David recognized he had collided with God. But rather than reducing David to a mere feather, God's heart wanted David's heart back. David was wise enough to embrace the promise of God, and he ran into the arms of hope rather than the blades of destruction.

October 13

"Again I say to you, that if two of you agree on earth about anything that they may ask, it shall be done for them by My Father who is in heaven."

MATTHEW 18:19

Prayer is a critical mission of the church as a corporate community. The church is sown into the fallen world as salt, and the preservative power for the sin-corrupted world is in the intercessions of God's people. When they are in conflict, there is cacophony, not concord. Their prayers are hindered. Conflict always stifles communion with God. His ears delight in a symphony, produced when all the instruments are in harmony. When people centered on His will cry out to Him in unity, God releases His blessings.

October 14

*"For where two or three have gathered together
in My name, I am there in their midst."*

MATTHEW 18:20

On the day of His ascension, Jesus' disciples gathered around and pressed in on Him. They attended His words with intense concentration. The closer they gathered around the One in their midst, the nearer they got to one another. It is so now. Whenever Christ's people assemble—be it a mere two or three—with Jesus at the center, the more they press in to Him, the closer they get to each other. Jesus is the core of Christian fellowship and community.

October 15

*Now on the last day, the great day of the feast,
Jesus stood and cried out, saying, "If anyone is thirsty,
let him come to Me and drink. He who believes
in Me, as the Scripture said, 'From his innermost being
will flow rivers of living water.'"*

JOHN 7:37-38

God promises overflow living. Some people function with their cups half full. Others get zest and energy for life almost to the brim. But God's indwelling life is different. The vessel of a human life cannot contain it all, and to be full of Him is to lavish the bounty on others. Whatever fills your bucket is what will slosh out on others. Drink deeply from His Spirit, and you will refresh everyone you touch.

October 16

For as many as are the promises of God, in Him they are yes.

2 CORINTHIANS 1:20

Dr. Chester Swor, one of the twentieth century's most inspiring speakers, said he was retiring. His body was lame and weary. "You can't do that!" I said. "You still have a message." I remembered E. Stanley Jones, who wrote in his eighties that all the promises of God are true. If God gave a message and a promise in one's youth, the promise still stands. The reason is that all the promises are deposited in Jesus Christ. As long as Christ lives— and that's forever—the promises stand. Chester Swor and E. Stanley Jones discovered afresh in their most senior years that Jesus and His promises are forever young.

"For God did not send the Son into the world to judge the world, but that the world might be saved through Him." . . . Christ Jesus, who is to judge the living and the dead.

JOHN 3:17; 2 TIMOTHY 4:1

A judge was driving to his court when a drunk driver suddenly veered off the road in front of him and smashed into a tree. The jurist jumped from his car and tried to rescue the man from his burning car. Instead, the uninjured drunk ran away. Police caught and arrested the drunk driver. Ironically, the man was brought before the very judge who tried to save him. In one venue, the judge had come to save him, but in another he was the man's judge. In His incarnation in the earth, Jesus came to save the world, but in eternity He sits as the world's judge.

October 18

He who dwells in the shelter of the Most High
Will abide in the shadow of the Almighty.
I will say to the LORD, "My refuge and my fortress,
My God, in whom I trust!"

PSALM 91:1–2

Anxiety disorders cost Americans more than $40 billion annually. Such fears manifest themselves in two ways—specific phobias, like fear of spiders or flying, and social phobias, such as fear of scrutiny, embarrassment, or humiliation in the eyes of others. We fear being exposed to threats, and we fear our flaws being exposed to other people. Lurking in every person's subconscious is the dread of ultimate exposure before God in judgment. But to be in God is to be inside the refuge nothing can penetrate.

"*Behold, I have given you authority to tread on serpents and scorpions, and over all the power of the enemy, and nothing will injure you.*"

LUKE 10:19

Almost all of Jesus' followers listening to this promise that day were injured under persecution and executed. Was Jesus lying to them? He Himself experienced the fiery baptism of the cross. Was He deluded? The promise is actually greater than we think. Authority is in relation to mission. Jesus promises the authority to war against the spiritual foe for the sake of God's Kingdom. The injury the adversary wants to bring is eternal torment, but he has no power to do so against those wielding Christ's authority as they are on their Kingdom mission.

October 20

The secret of the LORD is for those who fear Him,
And He will make them know His covenant.

PSALM 25:14

We don't contemplate the blessing of water until we're thirsty, or the nourishment of bread until hungry. Peter knew the covenant of grace only when his denial of Christ confronted him with his need. Saul of Tarsus didn't see his impoverishment until he was blinded on the Damascus Road. God is love, and love wants to be out in the open, not secretive. God brings us to the place we know His promises to us. We screech and scream, and then the tears evaporate when we know what He wants us to know—the depth of His love and the extent of His promises.

October 21

He who pursues righteousness and loyalty
Finds life, righteousness and honor.

PROVERBS 21:21

There's a profound difference between existence and life. The existentialist focuses only on the moment and its experience. But the person with life has rich, wonderful, meaningful being. The pursuit of righteousness—God's holy character—brings one into true being rather than mere existence. Such high living transforms one into a character like God's. Others recognize, admire, and honor this rich quality. Such people increasingly are like their Lord of whom it was said that not even His enemies could find evil to speak against Him.

Oelober 22

*But godliness actually is a means of great gain
when accompanied by contentment.*

1 TIMOTHY 6:6

Godliness is the greatest possession. The possibility of loss drives the worries that drain us of contentment. But when we fix our eyes on the greatest possession—the one that stands for eternity—and realize that it can never be lost, contentment results. In the eyes of God, we are declared godly the moment we trust Christ. In this world, transformation begins through His Spirit, giving us the experience of the godliness we already have in Him. "He is no fool who gives what he cannot keep to gain what he cannot lose," said Jim Elliott, before he was martyred in South America.[25]

October 23

There is no fear in love; but perfect love casts out fear,
because fear involves punishment,
and the one who fears is not perfected in love.

1 JOHN 4:18

The "fear of God" negatively is the terror of His punishment. Positively, to fear God is to revere, respect, honor, and adore Him as the Most High. One who understands God's perfect love, and whose love for Him is increasingly perfected, does not live in the dread of God's wrath. "Our God is a consuming fire" (Hebrews 12:29). For those who don't understand His perfect love, that fire represents the worst of terrors. But the people who receive the perfection of His love find the fire warming, energizing, and overwhelming the darkness.

October 24

The LORD ... will keep your soul.

PSALM 121:7

Keeping," or "preserving" is to exercise great care over an object of value. The soul is the seat of human personality, the source of thinking, emotions, and choosing. A Brinks truck bearing a load of cash stops at a bank to deposit its day's collection. Immediately, guards spring out and surround the vehicle. With gun drawn, a security officer carries the wealth into the bank. Leering eyes look on, wanting to grab the money. In the fallen world, the thief desires to snatch our souls, but God surrounds our minds, feelings, and volition with His great care.

"The steadfast of mind You will keep in perfect peace,
Because he trusts in You."

ISAIAH 26:3

Some types of anchors are designed with sturdy hooks to dig into a sea bottom or latch on to a big rock. They halt a boat's drag, caused by wind and waves. The soul needs to be anchored. Paul wrote that we are tossed about by winds and waves of differing beliefs (Ephesians 4:14). James describes the doubt that sometimes causes us to be driven on the surf of unbelief, and carried along with whatever wind may be blowing (James 1:6). But faith in God anchors the soul, stops the drift and drag, and enables us to rest even in stormy seas.

October 26

He stores up sound wisdom for the upright.

PROVERBS 2:7

God moved Joseph to build storehouses for the surplus of Egyptian grain, and when the famine came the food was available. Our world is data-rich, but there's a famine of wisdom. Every truth comes from God, but His covenant people are given more than mere data. He releases to and through them the wisdom to apply the information for good. Many in Egypt knew how to build silos, but Joseph had the wisdom to know why and when to construct the granaries.

October 27

*But if any of you lacks wisdom, let him
ask of God, who gives to all generously and without
reproach, and it will be given to him.*

JAMES 1:5

The key to God's wisdom storehouse is petitionary prayer. Those too proud to ask won't get the rich supply. To ask is to acknowledge one's need. Pride keeps us from asking. "Don't tell me how to drive!" I snapped at Jo Beth one day as we tried to take the shortest route and make a tight schedule. Later, while preparing to preach, I came face to face with my pride. But God promises that if we recognize our need, and from that humility ask for His wisdom, we will receive it in abundance.

October 28

"If my people, which are called by my name,
shall humble themselves, and pray,
and seek my face, and turn from their wicked ways;
then will I hear from heaven, and will forgive
their sin, and will heal their land."

2 CHRONICLES 7:14 KJV

Light radiates. An energy core illuminates all in
its range. God's "remnant people," those in
covenant with Him, bless their whole community
and world. As they humbly seek God for their
nation and society, and as they turn from their sin,
God heals the land. How does a nation repent?
Not all will see the need. But as the energy core of
God's people of promise repents for the sins of
society, God has mercy on the whole. The radiating
effect bathes everything around it with light.

October 29

He will remember His covenant forever.

PSALM 111:5

In September 1938, Hitler assured British Prime Minister Chamberlain that he would limit his conquests to the Sudetenland. In 1939, Hitler signed a nonaggression pact with the Soviets. Hitler broke both agreements, along with many others. But neither was Stalin faithful to his promises. World history is littered with shredded paper from pacts and agreements that meant nothing to the signers. But when God enters a covenant with us, He never forgets it or violates it.

October 30

The kingdom of God is not eating and drinking,
but righteousness and peace and joy in the Holy Spirit.

ROMANS 14:17

When tourists visit Las Vegas they are guaranteed lights, entertainment, and buffet tables. For many, this is the essence of living. Yet a headline in the *Las Vegas Sun* reads, "Experts grappling with high suicide rate."[26] The stark contradiction between promise and reality is too much for some. But to come into God's Kingdom is to enter a realm not dependent on glitter, glamour, and glut. Rather, God's Kingdom pulsates with Spirit-fired joy, rests in His peace, and has goodness as its atmosphere.

October 31

When you lie down, you will not be afraid;
When you lie down, your sleep will be sweet.

PROVERBS 3:24

Children cringe on Halloween, their nightmares full of ghouls banging at their doors and hiding under their beds. For many people, night-fears are chronic, not limited to Halloween. They awake in the night with anxieties, or toss with concerns. God's people can sleep peacefully. If a growling ghoul tries to awaken them with worry, they can the rest the fear in God, turn over, and go back to sleep.

November

❧

November 1

*Looking for the blessed hope and the appearing
of the glory of our great God and Savior, Christ Jesus.*

TITUS 2:13

All the richness of God's holy character is in His glory. It is the manifestation of His purity and beauty. Jesus Christ is the full expression of God's immaculate Being. Wherever He is in *His* fullness, the Godhead is present in fullness. That which has fallen short of the glory of God is brought to *its* fullness of purity when Jesus Christ is present—from individuals to the world itself. His appearing is the blessed hope of all.

November 2

All the earth will be filled with the glory of the LORD.

NUMBERS 14:21

G od delights in filling things. He filled the void
with His word and created the universes. He
breathed into a clay–lump, and it became a human
being. God fills a fallen person with His Holy Spirit,
and the man or woman becomes a new creation.
The devil tries to fill things with his presence,
believing he can block the habitation of God's Spirit.
But with the flick of a finger, Jesus banishes the
demons. When God's glory fills the earth, the devil
and his demonic host will be displaced, and the
whole world will reflect God's pure character.

Do not be afraid of sudden fear
Nor of the onslaught of the wicked when it comes;
For the LORD will be your confidence
And will keep your foot from being caught.

PROVERBS 3:25-26

Drum Castle, near Aberdeen, Scotland, has been restored to striking handsomeness. Outside are rich gardens of winding shrubs. It's pleasant on a Scottish spring day to stroll in the greenery. Many people see life like that. They ease through the garden until suddenly there's the onslaught of the enemy jumping from behind the shrubs. A terrifying phone call, squadrons of criticism, and looming defeat come seemingly from nowhere. God's promise to His covenant people is that if they will maintain their faith-grip on His faithfulness even in the suddenness of the ambush, they can face it with confidence.

November 4

"Peace I leave with you; My peace I give to you;
not as the world gives do I give to you. Do not let your
heart be troubled, nor let it be fearful."

JOHN 14:27

T he world's peace is negative, dependent on the absence of conflict. Jesus' peace is positive. He told His followers He hadn't come to bring peace, but a "sword" (Matthew 10:34). His very presence excited opposition and persecution. Yet in the midst of the strife, Jesus' disciples would have His peace. So Stephen dies under the stones of an angry mob, glorifying Jesus as he perishes. Eighty-six-year-old Polycarp, a faithful follower, refuses to deny Jesus and burns at the stake, declaring his friendship with the Lord to the end. And so it has gone for centuries—people experiencing Christ's peace in the midst of their blood, sweat, and tears.

November 5

*"But I tell you the truth, it is to your advantage that
I go away; for if I do not go away, the Helper will
not come to you; but if I go, I will send Him to you."*

JOHN 16:7

I'm always a little suspicious of people who start
out saying, "Now this is the truth . . ." But Jesus
knew this would be difficult for His disciples to
believe. "It's to your advantage I go away." He had
told them of their future suffering, and now He
seems to say He won't be around. But later they
discover the advantage. In His physical body, He
couldn't be with them in Judea when He was in
Galilee. But through His Holy Spirit, Jesus would
be with His suffering people wherever they may be
and in whatever era they live, including the
twenty-first century.

November 6

"If you then, being evil, know how to give good gifts to your children, how much more will your heavenly Father give the Holy Spirit to those who ask Him?"

LUKE 11:13

We get as much of God as we desire to get. It's not enough merely to say, "I wish I really knew Jesus Christ," or, "I want victory over shame and sin." We can *wish* and we can *want*, but it's not until we *will* that we receive the Father's best for us. We yearn as if He were reluctant to give us His good gifts. He has willed to give us His best, and when our will meets His will, His best is what we get. Wishing and wanting are passive, but willing is active because it asks, seeks, and knocks.

*"'For I will pour out water on the thirsty land
And streams on the dry ground;
I will pour out My Spirit on your offspring
And My blessing on your descendants;
And they will spring up among the grass
Like poplars by streams of water.'"*

ISAIAH 44:3-4

Texas Hill Country ranchers dig long, shallow trenches called "draws" leading down to their ponds, or "tanks," which nestle at the land's lowest places. When summers are dry, they delight in the "gully washers" that dump rain into the draws, and they watch with glee as the water fills up the tanks where cattle can drink. God promises His people gully washers. Just about the time we are thirstiest, driest, and most needy, He pours His Spirit upon us. We then touch our families with God's refreshing so that they, too, can enjoy His rich flow.

Therefore, having been justified by faith,
we have peace with God through our Lord Jesus Christ,
through whom also we have obtained our
introduction by faith into this grace in which we stand;
and we exult in hope of the glory of God.

ROMANS 5:1-2

Prior to being reconciled—or "made one with"—God, we are at war, "enmity," with Him (Romans 8:7; James 4:4). When peace is established, war is over. Jesus gives us peace with God, ending our state of enmity against Him. "I've made my peace with God," some say as they contemplate death. But humans don't establish that peace. An armistice in which no one wins is not true peace. Peace comes when there is a victor. Jesus conquered the enmity at the cross and reconciled us to the Father. We are at peace with God in Christ.

November 9

*And not only this, but we also exult in
our tribulations, knowing that tribulation brings about
perseverance; and perseverance, proven character;
and proven character, hope.*

ROMANS 5:3-4

"Exult" means being "excited." How can we be
excited in tribulations? Paul is no masochist,
relishing pain, but he sees where tribulation leads.
His eyes are stretched out to God's view of things,
not the human perspective. For the person whose
life belongs to God, there are no dead ends. Every
road leads somewhere, even the rocky, dangerous,
narrow paths. Paul has learned in his engagement
with God that tribulation leads to staying power
and that staying power proves the quality of one's
character, and this knowledge sparks hope that
people can meet successfully every challenge
through God's power.

November 10

> *Hope does not disappoint, because the love*
> *of God has been poured out within our hearts through*
> *the Holy Spirit who was given to us.*

ROMANS 5:5

Hope and love are connected like heart and lungs. When breathing becomes stressed and comes in troubled gasps, the heart keeps pulsating. Spiritually, when we are constricted and pressured, the Holy Spirit reminds us with the constancy of a beating heart that God's love is overseeing it all. If you "hope" to win millions in a lottery you're likely to be disappointed. The Greek word for "hope" used in Romans means anticipation with expectancy. That means when we pass through suffering we expect to discover in its hardships the manifestation of His love.

November 11

My flesh and my heart may fail,
But God is the strength of my heart
and my portion forever.

PSALM 73:26

A house-moving company was asked to transfer a three-story brick building from one location to another. The workers split the structure from its foundations, then inserted girders. But the steel beams couldn't do the lifting without massive jacks that hoisted the building. Our physical structure wasn't designed for heavy lifting. But God is the power supporting us, and through His strength we can bear heavy loads. Sometimes His people look back and say, "Only through God could I have made it through that!"

Say among the nations, "The LORD reigns;
Indeed, the world is firmly established."

PSALM 96:10

A friend stepped off a plane in a strife-torn nation and said it felt as if the very atmosphere was trembling. He fought panic, wanting to run back up the steps of the aircraft and zoom out of the place. But then my associate remembered that God ultimately reigns over all. The devil has usurped power temporarily in the fallen world, but Almighty God's hand steadies the world and someday will again manifest His reign everywhere. The world is firmly established in His plan, and not even the devil's rebellion can bring it down to hell with him.

*And without faith it is impossible to please Him,
for he who comes to God must believe that He is and
that He is a rewarder of those who seek Him.*

HEBREWS 11:6

What about the people who've never heard of Christ and the gospel?" The promise of God is that when an individual is obedient to the light he or she has, God will provide more light and lead the person to opportunity to know Christ. Take Cornelius. He was a Roman soldier living in Caesarea who loved the true God and wanted to know Him. In a simultaneous act, God prepared Cornelius to receive Simon Peter and Simon Peter to reach out to a non-Jew. God rewarded Cornelius the seeker with all for which his heart had yearned.

*At the name of Jesus every knee will bow, of those
who are in heaven and on earth and under the earth,
and that every tongue will confess that
Jesus Christ is Lord, to the glory of God the Father.*

PHILIPPIANS 2:10–11

The bowing and confessing have already started. When the ascended Jesus entered Heaven, the archangels, cherubim, and seraphim bowed and proclaimed Him Lord. Someday every knee "on earth" will bow and some will say, "Oh No! Jesus *is* Lord!" while others shout, "Hallelujah! *Jesus is* Lord!" The tumult of acclamation will pour over into Hell, and even Satan and the fallen angels swarming around him will fall to their knees and "preach" the message they've resisted from the foundations of the world—"*Jesus is Lord!*"

November 15

*For I am not ashamed of the gospel, for it is
the power of God for salvation to everyone who believes,
to the Jew first and also to the Greek.*

ROMANS 1:16

I 'm proud of the Gospel," says Paul (Moffet Translation). When I'm proud of what I can do without God, it positions me like a raft trying to go upstream in gushing rapids. But when I'm proud of the transforming work of the Gospel in my life and others, I'm flowing in the mighty river of God, buoyed by His surge. My pride says I can change myself, but humility says only Jesus Christ can transform me. I have no grounds for personal pride, but I do have immense reason to be proud of *His* power, declared in the Good News of Jesus Christ.

November 16

A righteous man who walks in his integrity—
How blessed are his sons after him.

PROVERBS 20:7

The military officer sat in a prison camp. "You have one hour to live," his captors told him, "and one letter to write." The POW penned one sentence to his son. "Dear Bill, the word is integrity." The young man wouldn't have his father during critical formative years, but he had his dad's character going before him. The son was blessed. Integrity is a handsome garment, woven of who you are when no one is watching, what you stand for, and the name you carry. Integrity is among the greatest riches we can pass to our children.

Though I walk in the midst of trouble, You will revive me.

PSALM 138:7

John F. Kennedy wrote the acclaimed book *Profiles in Courage*. Sometimes we are "living books" that might be rightly titled *Profiles in Trouble*. You know the distinctive marks: baggy eyes, somber demeanor, taut speech, sagging shoulders, and a drooping walk. Trouble is a drainer. Revival is the renewal of strength and passion for living. The soul is to the body what a big engine room is to a ship in that the soul houses the spirit, which is the engine. Revival is God's Spirit reigniting the human spirit, resulting in vitality, even when we're a walking profile of trouble.

Jesus answered and said to her, "Everyone who drinks
of this water will thirst again; but whoever
drinks of the water that I will give him shall never
thirst; but the water that I will give him will become in
him a well of water springing up to eternal life."

JOHN 4:13–14

I n *The Last Crusade* Major V. Gilbert tells of the
early twentieth-century battle for Palestine
against the Turks.[27] At one point allied forces
outpaced the camel caravan bearing their water.
Thirst became maddening, but there were wells at
Sheria, which was occupied by the enemy. "We
fought that day as men fight for their lives," Gilbert
wrote. He concluded, "If such were our thirst for
God and for righteousness, for His will in our life, a
consuming, all-embracing, pre-occupying desire,
how rich in the fruit of the spirit would we be."

November 19

Therefore we do not lose heart,
but though our outer man is decaying, yet our
inner man is being renewed day by day.

2 CORINTHIANS 4:16

There are exceptional people whose bodies are weary with age but whose spirits dance with childlike freshness. What we take in day by day in our younger years determines our inner vitality in later life. We are in old age what we have been all along. Live daily in God's joy and peace when you're younger, and joy and peace will be your character when you are gray-haired. Resisting decay in natural objects is futile. However, for the human spirit alive with God's life, there is no decay, only a constancy of renewal until the grand consummation of joy and peace when we meet Christ in His glory.

November 20

*For momentary, light affliction is producing for us an
eternal weight of glory far beyond all comparison.*

2 CORINTHIANS 4:17

Grapes or olives were placed in a round stone
trough, and a massive rock crushed out the
rich oil. The heavy stone was, in Greek, *thlipsis*, the
word translated "tribulation." God's covenant
people cannot lose—even in tribulation. Its crushing
weight becomes the means by which Christ's
followers flow with the best. Grapes became
refreshing wine and oil provided light. God's people
under pressure provide encouragement and
illumination to all around them.

November 21

For everything created by God is good, and nothing is to be rejected if it is received with gratitude; for it is sanctified by means of the word of God and prayer.

1 TIMOTHY 4:4-5

Sanctification isn't a religious car wash. Pass through a grinding, scrubbing washing machine and the mud comes off. The car comes out on the other side glimmering. Sanctification, however, is the process by which God sets things apart for the use He intended. He created all things to fulfill His purposes. They are corrupted by human sin. But when God recovers them He restores them to His high aims. And that includes human beings soured and dirtied by sin.

November 22

We give thanks to You, O God, we give thanks,
For Your name is near.

PSALM 75:1

Two barbers, one godly, one vile, worked side by side. One day the pastor came for a haircut, but the rude guy was missing. "He's sick and in a coma," the godly barber said. But weeks later the pastor heard someone call his name at the post office. It was the crude barber, who now gleamed. "I was in a coma," the man explained, "but I could hear the doctor whispering to my wife I wouldn't last an hour. For the first time in sixty years I cried out to God to help me. "Would you believe it? When I called His name, He came near."

November 23

*Be anxious for nothing, but in everything by prayer
and supplication with thanksgiving let your requests
be made known to God. And the peace of God, which
surpasses all comprehension, will guard your hearts
and your minds in Christ Jesus.*

PHILIPPIANS 4:6-7

Nirvana, a concept in several Oriental religions, is the state of detachment from all pain and concerns, which translates ultimately to turning off the capacity to interact with the wound–giving world. "Anxious for nothing" doesn't mean *Nirvana*. Christ's followers are called to be engaged with stark daily reality, not withdraw. Rather, to be "anxious for nothing" means that we are not to worry constantly, or keep revisiting concerns in our minds. As we live in the fury of the world, turning over our fears and scars to God, His peace guards us.

November 29

*"He who offers a sacrifice of thanksgiving honors Me;
And to him who orders his way aright
I shall show the salvation of God."*

PSALM 50:23

Seeing the salvation of God isn't watching a cheap sideshow. Sign-seekers in Jesus' day wanted to see strange sights and be entertained with miracles. Seeing the salvation of God means observing the outcomes of commitment to Him. A missionary heard of an African sorcerer who could turn men into elephants, and the missionary was intimidated. "I can't do that," he fretted. Then the missionary realized that it's nothing to reduce a human being to a lower order in a fallen world. The real miracle is a sinful person made Christlike. That's seeing the salvation of God.

November 25

O give thanks to the LORD, for He is good;
For His lovingkindness is everlasting.

1 CHRONICLES 16:34

Divorce hurts all concerned. It especially hurts God's heart. Divorce interrupts the flow of love and kindness between two people. Many couples attempt an amicable separation, but it's hard to keep out the strife that ended the marriage in the first place. God never divorces His covenant people. We may wound His heart, and even pass through seasons when our ways aren't compatible with His, but He doesn't break off the relationship. He works and waits patiently for our return, because His lovingkindness is everlasting.

*Thanks be to God, who gives us the victory
through our Lord Jesus Christ.*

1 CORINTHIANS 15:57

The moment in 1944 the Allies landed on Normandy's beaches, Hitler was finished. However, it took another eleven months to bring the victory to the bunker where the Nazi tyrant hid. The moment Jesus Christ was born, Satan was defeated. The Kingdom of God arrived in Jesus, and we live in the era when that victory is advancing in the world. The full impact of Christ's victory will be evident in His Second Coming. Meanwhile, His people are moving in the wake of the victory He's already won.

Now may the God of peace Himself sanctify you entirely; and may your spirit and soul and body be preserved complete, without blame at the coming of our Lord Jesus Christ. Faithful is He who calls you, and He also will bring it to pass.

1 THESSALONIANS 5:23-24

The human spirit enables God-consciousness, the soul self-consciousness, and the body world-consciousness. However, God's design is for us to function as whole beings, not fragmented. Sin shatters the wholeness. Paul's lament in Romans 7 and Galatians 5 is the warfare this fragmentation produces between the "flesh" and the "spirit." Christ's salvation restores wholeness to the human being. He does the work and brings it to fruition. Through Christ, we are brought back to God's perfect design.

November 28

"Be strong and courageous, do not be afraid or tremble at them, for the LORD your God is the one who goes with you. He will not fail you or forsake you."

DEUTERONOMY 31:6

The only way to get to the site that is most likely the actual place Jesus was baptized is to traverse a no-man's land laced with mines. A narrow road leads down to the Jordan. On rare occasions, scholars and tourists may be taken there, but only in the company of Israeli soldiers and their guns. In life, we walk through minefields and become surrounded by enemies. But God's promise is to be our armed escort. If we go in company with Him, we don't have to tremble at the dangers around us.

November 29

And my God will supply all your needs
according to His riches in glory in Christ Jesus.

PHILIPPIANS 4:19

God always knows the true needs of His covenant people. At one point the Hebrews in the wilderness thought they needed the onions, leeks, and garlic of Egypt, but God knew they needed manna. They fretted over getting new shoes for the rugged Sinai, but God knew they needed their old ones to stay new. The people murmured that they needed water when all they could see was rocks, but God knew they needed the water in the rock. We can trust God to supply our needs, not our preferences or the misguided wishes we bring with us from the land that enslaved us.

November 30

"I am the vine, you are the branches;
he who abides in Me and I in him, he bears much fruit,
for apart from Me you can do nothing."

JOHN 15:5

We either bear the fruit of the spirit or the fruit of the flesh. The fruit of the thorn bush is thorns—"immorality, impurity, sensuality, idolatry, sorcery, enmities, strife, jealousy, outbursts of anger, disputes, dissensions, factions, envying, drunkenness, carousing" (Galatians 5:19–21) But the fruit of the Spirit is "love, joy, peace, patience, kindness, goodness, faithfulness, gentleness, self-control" (Galatians 5:22–23). Those rooted in the thorn bush bristle with thorns, but those who dwell in Christ bear true fruit.

December

December 1

The LORD God said to the serpent,
"Because you have done this,
Cursed are you....
He shall bruise you on the head."

GENESIS 3:14–15

In earth's early morning, God promises He will send a Deliverer. The serpent backed humanity into a corner, and the biological father of the race—Adam—took the wrong way out, trapping all his descendants in his choice. But God, who sees the panorama of all time, tells the serpent and promises humanity that, although the slithering snake will inflict a non-deadly wound on the Deliverer, the Promised One would crush the serpent's head, smashing his authority and power. All history is a buildup to this promise, and all history after the Deliverer comes is a buildup to the establishment of His Kingdom universally.

December 2

Then a shoot will spring from the stem of Jesse,
And a branch from his roots will bear fruit.
The Spirit of the LORD will rest on Him,
The spirit of wisdom and understanding,
The spirit of counsel and strength,
The spirit of knowledge and the fear of the LORD.

ISAIAH 11:1–2

The promised Deliverer will be the One on whom the Spirit of God rests. "Anointing" is the term used to describe the Holy Spirit's "coming upon" a person. Thus, the Deliverer will be The Anointed One—*Messiah* from the Hebrew language and *Christos* from the Greek. The completeness of the Holy Spirit will be upon the Promised One. He will be the appearing in the created world of all God is, and He will have all God's authority and resting on and operating within Himself.

December 3

*"Therefore the Lord Himself will give you a sign:
Behold, a virgin will be with child and bear a son,
and she will call His name Immanuel."*

ISAIAH 7:14

The Deliverer upon whom the Spirit rests will
have no sin. Otherwise, He wouldn't be qualified
to crush the head of the serpent, but instead would
be under the serpent's head. A sin-imprisoned man
cannot set others free from sin. His qualifications
for atoning for humanity's sin will rest on the purity
of His life. Therefore, the Deliverer is born of a
virgin. The contaminated seed of Adam won't be in
Him. And when the virgin names Him she will
recognize Him as the Promised One. She will call
Him "God-With-Us," Immanuel.

December 4

"But as for you, Bethlehem Ephrathah,
Too little to be among the clans of Judah,
From you One will go forth for Me to be ruler in Israel.
His goings forth are from long ago,
From the days of eternity."

MICAH 5:2

The Promised Deliverer will be born in Bethlehem, Micah prophesies more than six hundred years before the event. The One who will be the Bread of Life comes from the "House of Bread," which is what "Bethlehem" means. Ancient peoples marked Bethlehem as being in a fertile region, rich in grain. The Old Testament is a trail of crumbs leading to the Bread of Life. God gives clear clues so that people can recognize the true Messiah when He comes—even down to the place where He will be born. The Father doesn't want us to miss His Son, the Promised One.

December 5

For a child will be born to us, a son will be given to us;
And the government will rest on His shoulders;
And His name will be called Wonderful Counselor,
Mighty God,
Eternal Father, Prince of Peace.

ISAIAH 9:6

Government restrains the chaos the serpent lets loose in the world. But government, too, can be caught in the deadly vortex if it has the wrong foundation. Law easily slides into force and tyranny. The only hope for liberty in a world gone mad is government based on love and grace. The Promised One will come bearing the government of the Kingdom of God. As Wonderful Counselor, Mighty God, and Eternal Father, He will be strong enough to restrain evil, but gentle enough to be the Prince of Peace.

December 6

The people who walk in darkness
Will see a great light;
Those who live in a dark land,
The light will shine on them.

ISAIAH 9:2

The deeper the darkness, the brighter the light appears. Light a match in a deep cavern and it is a torch. It is those drenched in darkness who receive the shining light. When sin tightens its clutch, when misery becomes a darkening cloak, when oppression, sickness, poverty, and despair close in like opaque walls, God sends His Light into the world. Those who prefer flickers to flame will not see the light. But people existing in the dark shadows yearn for the brilliance, and God will give it to them.

December 7

"The scepter shall not depart from Judah,
Nor the ruler's staff from between his feet,
Until Shiloh comes,
And to him shall be the obedience of the peoples."

GENESIS 49:10

"S hiloh" is coming, God promises. The Peacemaker will appear in history, rising from the Tribe of Judah, David's clan. Shiloh comes and makes peace possible between people and God, through His reconciling atonement. But the scepter and ruler's staff will remain in the world until Shiloh comes to establish peace between humans and all their adversarial relationships. Then a child will play at the hole of the scorpion, and swords will be beaten into plowshares. The sequence of peacemaking is first peace between people and God, then peace between humans and nature. Shiloh has come and is coming.

December 8

"The LORD your God will raise up for you
a prophet like me from among you, from your
countrymen, you shall listen to him."

DEUTERONOMY 18:15

Moses was a frontier man. He led Israel to the frontiers of the Promised Land and established the era of Law. The Promised Prophet is, like Moses, a frontier Man. He leads God's covenant people to a new land of promise, His Kingdom. Further, the Promised One forges a new era that supplants Law—the Year of God's favor, the era of Grace. Moses stands astride history past; the Promised Prophet, the Messiah, towers over history past, present, and future. He cuts the path across the frontiers, making it possible for human beings to pass into the presence of God.

December 9

A voice is calling,
"Clear the way for the LORD in the wilderness;
Make smooth in the desert a highway for our God."

ISAIAH 40:3

God promises the Calling Voice to herald Messiah's appearing. We will know the Promised One because the Calling Voice will alert us. The hearing of God's words fades after centuries of dynamic exchange between Heaven and earth. Four silent centuries creep by. Battles rage, Masada falls, the temple is desecrated and Israel mourns. Then a voice thunders in the desert arroyos and along the lush riverbanks. The Calling Voice is right on time. Its culminating words are, "Behold, the Lamb of God, who takes away the sin of the world!"

He says, "It is too small a thing that
You should be My Servant
To raise up the tribes of Jacob and
to restore the preserved ones of Israel;
I will also make You a light of the nations
So that My salvation may reach to the end of the earth."

ISAIAH 49:6

Mighty kings didn't know it, but the bottom-up revolution was shaping deep in the bosom of history, and they were merely bit players. What God began with a people at the bottom of the social, economic, and political scale would progress through His Promised One until the whole world heard of Israel's—and the world's—Deliverer. He Himself would declare: "This gospel of the kingdom shall be preached in the whole world as a testimony to all the nations, and then the end will come" (Matthew 24:14).

December 11

But He was pierced through for our transgressions,
He was crushed for our iniquities;
The chastening for our well-being fell upon Him,
And by His scourging we are healed.

ISAIAH 53:5

The person who says he has no problems is not telling the truth. God has not called us to live in deceit and fantasy. A mere confession that we are problem-free is not biblical faith, but delusion. What we are free to confess if we are in covenant with Christ is that there is not a need we have, problem we face, crisis we encounter or dread looming before us that has not been dealt with in the atonement of Jesus Christ. How, when, and where He manifests the outcome to us is His business. Ours is to celebrate what Christ has done in bearing all our iniquities on Himself.

December 12

All of us like sheep have gone astray,
Each of us has turned to his own way;
But the LORD has caused the iniquity of us all
To fall on Him.

ISAIAH 53:6

I don't particularly like sheep. I never heard of one being strong or doing anything heroic. Some people prefer the ancient Greek humanist idea that sinning shows courage to rebel against the gods. Sin is a fall uphill, they think. But sin actually is a deadly plunge, and ignoring it leads to death. Sin is rebellion against our true nature. God is grieved, but we are damaged severely when we stray. That's why Jesus took on our sin. He invites us to let all our pain be His. If that takes being a helpless sheep, then one would be a fool not to delight in the role.

December 13

"*For that which refers to Me has its fulfillment.*"

LUKE 22:37

There is a progression throughout the prophecies leading to Jesus Christ. In Genesis, God promises the One who will crush the serpent's head will be of the human race. Through Abraham, God identifies the nation through which Messiah will come. God shows Jacob the tribe, Judah. In His promises to David, God reveals the Deliverer's family line. Through Micah, God indicates the Messiah's hometown. Isaiah is shown the type of mother who will bear Immanuel. Like a cinematographer, God slowly zooms in the lens of prophecy until Jesus Christ fills the screen of History.

December 14

Jesus said to them, "I am the bread of life;
he who comes to Me will not hunger, and he who
believes in Me will never thirst.

JOHN 6:35

The best humans could do until Jesus came was, like Solomon in Ecclesiastes, lament their hunger and look forward to a feast. And when the banquet table was set, many disbelieved the bounty and passed it by. Religious people always say that grace is too good to be true. They have to bring something to the table—ceremony, ritual, scholarship, titles, credentials. They are like a gracious lady invited to dinner who inquires, "What can I bring?" But Jesus is the whole feast. "Just bring your appetite," He answers.

"I am the Light of the world; he who follows Me will not walk in the darkness, but will have the Light of life."

JOHN 8:12

Deacon Stephen looked up at Heaven and saw the glory of God as stones battered the life from his body. Pharisee Saul, who cheered Stephen's death, looked up into Heaven on the Damascus Road, and was plunged into the darkness of blindness. One man looked into the Light and saw, the other gazed into the brilliance, and couldn't see. Sometimes in His mercy God blinds us until we can really see, as in the case of Saul. And then we look into His Light and behold the glory of God, like Stephen.

"I am the door; if anyone enters through Me, he will be saved, and will go in and out and find pasture."

JOHN 10:9

To form a sheepfold, a shepherd stacked a stone wall or wove together thorn bushes. Then he lay down across a little passageway, literally becoming the door to the sheepfold. Jesus said the sheep go in and out. They dwell in security, go out to feed on the lush pastures, and return again to the safety of the fold, always passing through the door—the shepherd. The way to the lush grass and back again into the resting place was through the door—the shepherd. Jesus, our Shepherd, is the door to God and all His blessings.

*"I am the good shepherd; the good shepherd
lays down His life for the sheep."*

JOHN 10:11

For," in Greek, means "in place of." The wolf
enters, and the shepherd becomes the lamb the
predator wants to eat. This is why Jesus, the Good
Shepherd, is also the Lamb of God. It doesn't mean
Jesus is God's cuddly pet, but that Jesus stands in
our place. When the predator prowls and licks his
chops with us in view, Jesus rushes into the
destroyer's line of vision. At the cross, Jesus was
ravaged in our place. The wages of sin always is
death, and if someone doesn't collect the wage for
us, we must. The atonement is Jesus, the Lamb of
God, being sacrificed on our behalf.

*"Do you say of Him, whom the Father sanctified
and sent into the world, 'You are blaspheming,'
because I said, 'I am the Son of God'?"*

JOHN 10:36

Jesus, the Son, promises us sonship. Jesus is the
"only begotten" of the Father, meaning He is the
only one dressed in human flesh who was directly
sired by the Father. Yet Jesus Christ is fully God,
eternal with the Father. Because He is the only
Son, all the Father's treasures belong to Him.
When Jesus brings us into His sonship, we are one
with Him, and, therefore, heirs to all the promises
given to the Son of God. It would be as if Rockefeller
had only one child—you—making you heir to all
his fortune.

"I am the resurrection and the life; he who believes in
Me will live even if he dies, and everyone who lives and
believes in Me will never die. Do you believe this?"

JOHN 11:25-26

In Greek, *bios* refers often in the Bible to structural
life, existence in space and time. It is temporary.
Zoe frequently expresses the God-quality of life,
eternal and pure. *Bios* is finite—limited. *Zoe* is
infinite—unbounded by space and time. Our *bios*
structures are intended as the temple of God, for
His indwelling *Zoe*, through His Spirit. Prior to
receiving Christ, the temple is empty. When we
receive Christ, the Holy Spirit indwells us, making
us alive with His *Zoe*. Yet our bodies are still *bios*
structures and will decline and die. Someday we
will have a new body, perfectly aligned with the *Zoe*
that is our very life.

December 20

"I am the way, and the truth, and the life;
no one comes to the Father but through Me."

JOHN 14:6

Among those who believe all roads lead to Heaven
are Mr. Relativist, Mr. Pluralist, and Mr.
Universalist. The relativist says there is no absolute
truth, the pluralist argues that all truths are
equally absolute, and the universalist thinks it
doesn't matter because it's all going to work out.
Jesus says there's only way to the Father—through
Him. Jesus declares He is the incarnation of
absolute truth. Jesus identifies Himself as the
Zoe-life of God, invading the earth. He silences
Mr. Relativist with His assertion of absolute truth,
Mr. Pluralist with the distinctiveness of His life,
and Mr. Universalist with His one way to the Father.

December 21

"I am the true vine, and My Father is the vinedresser."

JOHN 15:1

How does a stingy person become generous, a fiery-tempered individual cool, and a proud person humble? We could visit the self-help section of a book store and survey titles offering personal transformation through ten steps or two, eighteen principles or perhaps twelve. The "spirituality" section offers the latest change techniques from gurus made famous on pop TV. But Jesus puts it simply. If we want to be transformed, we must connect to Him. No steps, no magic, no mantras or secret rituals, just relationship with the Cosmic Person who became a Concrete Person.

Behold, the Lord GOD will come with might....
Like a shepherd He will tend His flock,
In His arm He will gather the lambs.

ISAIAH 40:10–11

How fitting that the news about the coming of the Good Shepherd should be given first to shepherds, "abiding in the field, keeping watch over their flocks by night" (Luke 2:8). That's what it means for shepherds to tend their sheep. They dwell with the sheep, in the field, and the Good Shepherd comes into the world where we live. Shepherds guard their sheep, and Jesus keeps watch over His people continuously. Shepherds do this even in the night so that no predators creep under the darkness. Jesus tends the "sheep of His pasture" (Psalm 100:3) in the deep dark, and the destroyer cannot steal us away when our world turns to night.

December 23

"Then the glory of the LORD will be revealed,
And all flesh will see it together"....
And the Word became flesh, and dwelt among us, and
we saw His glory, glory as of the only begotten from the
Father, full of grace and truth.

ISAIAH 40:5; JOHN 1:14

If Jesus physically walked into a church, stadium, or some other assembly, many people believe the audience would stand and clap and shout. Not so. We would run and hide. We would be mortified in the face of the brilliant glory, the *Shekinah* in Hebrew. Three of Jesus' disciples beheld the glory for a moment on the Mount of Transfiguration. For a brief time, the physical garment was dropped, and they saw Him as He is. Someday all flesh will see Jesus in His full splendor. The appearance will be terrifying to those not cleansed by His blood, but a welcome sight to those who've given Him their lives.

386

But when the fullness of the time came, God sent forth His Son, born of a woman, born under the Law, so that He might redeem those who were under the Law, that we might receive the adoption as sons.

GALATIANS 4:4-5

When everything was prepared, when the full number of predictions and prophecies had come, when every type and symbol pointing to the Lamb and His blood had been laid into history's view, when the seed of Abraham had brought forth Jacob and Jacob's progeny had sired David, and David's family line had led to Mary and Joseph, and Mary and Joseph had been forced by a taxing government to Bethlehem, God pronounced history's cup full, and the Promised Messiah entered the world.

December 25

"For God so loved the world, that He gave
His only begotten Son, that whoever believes in Him
shall not perish, but have eternal life."

JOHN 3:16

When I was asked to preach a trial sermon at
the church I have now served almost three
decades, I refused. "Every preacher has two good
sermons, so I will do something different," I told
the search committee. When I stood to preach,
I quoted John 3:16, and stopped. "That's it?"
someone asked. Yes, that's "*it*." That simple truth is
the totality of the Bible. Everything in its 66
books, 1,189 chapters, 30,442 verses and 845,000
words is summed up in the sublime revelation that
God gave His Son to atone for our sins.

December 26

*God, . . . in these last days has spoken to us
in His Son, whom He appointed heir of all things,
through whom also He made the world.*

HEBREWS 1:1–2

Jesus Christ is the final, completive, summative and total word. For 1,500 years, God's Word came through the patriarchs and prophets. Thirty-nine Bible books resulted. But they could only give fragments of truth. The parts were there, scattered about like the components of a motor in an auto repair shop. But the combustion chamber was missing. The part that would bring energy and give meaning to all the other components wasn't there. Then, when Jesus Christ came into the world, everything was present and pulled together in Him. No longer was the truth of the Old Covenant fragmentary and incomplete, but united and powerful.

December 27

*And He is the radiance of His glory and
the exact representation of His nature, and upholds
all things by the word of His power.
When He had made purification of sins, He sat down
at the right hand of the Majesty on high, having
become as much better than the angels,
as He has inherited a more excellent name than they.*

HEBREWS 1:3–4

Years ago I spent the night in the Smoky
Mountains in a sleeping bag. I arose before the
sun was up, and in the darkness could see a scattering
of snow. I shivered in the cold. Then the sun came up,
and I watched its rays stroll gently through the trees.
The snow melted, and I was warmed. It reminded
me of Jesus. Though the analogy fails ultimately, He
is to the Father what sunbeams are to the sun. He is
the light that casts out the darkness, and He brings
warmth and energy to His children.

He is before all things,
and in Him all things hold together.

COLOSSIANS 1:17

Where's the 'missing matter'?" That's the question physics has asked for decades. There seems not to be enough matter in the universe to hold it together, yet there is cohesion. Jesus Christ is the One holding everything together. Body, soul, and spirit exist in a world caught in the spiritual gravity and entropy of a fallen system. Powerful forces pull at them, disintegrating the human being. But to the extent Jesus Christ is allowed to reign in a human heart, He holds all the facets of the human being together in wholeness. He keeps us from flying apart.

Behold, I tell you a mystery; we will not all sleep,
but we will all be changed, in a moment,
in the twinkling of an eye, at the last trumpet;
for the trumpet will sound, and the dead will be
raised imperishable, and we will be changed.

1 CORINTHIANS 15:51-52

Change and personal improvement are bywords of our day. Laws and rules are methods some try to produce transformation. But in Jesus Christ, change is guaranteed to occur. It's the difference between a rowboat and a sailboat. A person can row until the last trumpet sounds and not get to Heaven. But all the sailboat has to do is ride the wind. The wind, spiritually, is the Spirit of God, given by Jesus Christ. Let His wind fill your sails, and when the last trumpet sounds it will herald not only His coming, but your homecoming.

December 30

*"If I go and prepare a place for you,
I will come again and receive you to Myself,
that where I am, there you may be also.*

JOHN 14:3

Almost every Sunday at our church, we dedicate babies to the Lord. The wiggly creatures are dressed in their finest, held delicately by beaming parents. The little ones slept the night before in a room carefully prepared for them, full of color and happy things. This is what the Father does for His children. If you are in Christ, your special room is prepared and waiting. Death is merely a walk down the hall, a transfer from one room in God's cosmos to your quarters. And He holds your hand all the way.

"Truly I say to you, that you who have followed Me,
in the regeneration when the Son of Man will
sit on His glorious throne, you also shall
sit upon twelve thrones, judging the twelve tribes of Israel."

MATTHEW 19:28

P alingenesia, regeneration, is the destination of the promises of God. The term comes from the Greek words for "again" and "birth." The New Birth of the individual human through Jesus Christ leads them into the new birth of the whole cosmos. Simon Peter speaks of the "restoration of all things" (Acts 3:21), meaning the placing of everything into its original state. God's great plan for the world and everything that is in Him is to return it to the bliss of Paradise, when all things were in perfect harmony with Him and His ways. That's your destination, if you are in Christ and share the covenant of His promise.

Notes

Grateful acknowledgment is made to the following publishers for permission to reprint this copyrighted material.

1 John Piper, *Desiring God*, Sisters, Oregon: Multnomah, page 23.

2 "Barbara Bush's Most Embarrassing Moment" Retrieved from http://politicalhumor.about.com/library/jokes/ bljokebarbarabush.htm.

3 *Spurgeon's Daily Devotional*, PC Study Bible, Biblesoft. Emphasis in the original.

4 Larry Crabb, *Inside Out*, NavPress, 1988.

5 2 Corinthians 11:25-26, author's paraphrase.

6 "God's Outrageous Claims Unlocking Our Power," Sermon preached by Lee Strobel at Second Baptist Church, Houston, May 26, 2003.

7 "Hawking says humans close to finding answers to origins of universe," AFP, June 15, 2006. Retrieved from http://www.breitbart.com/news/2006/06/15/060615121526.oz37mqn8 .html.

8 Robert Jastrow, *God and the Astronomers*, page 116.

9 "No Longer An Enemy," By Paul W. Brubaker. Retrieved from http://www.brfwitness.org/Bread/noenemy.htm.

10 Retrieved from *http://www.christianquotes.org/ results.php*.

11 "Brightest Object in Universe Observed By University of Washington Astronomer," *Nature*, June 11, 1998. Retrieved from http://www.sciencedaily.com/ releases/1998/06/980616064401.htm.

[12] *Newsweek,* May 7, 2001.

[13] Woodrow Wilson (1856–1924). Letter, January 7, 1912, to Mary H.P. Hulbert. *The Public Papers of Woodrow Wilson.*

[14] Andrei Amalrik, *Will the Soviet Union Survive Until 1984?* New York: Harper Colophon Books, 1970.

[15] "Happiness lessons for all," By Sophie Goodchild, *The Independent,* July 9, 2006.

[16] Retrieved from http://www.religion-online.org/showarticle.asp?title=1658.

[17] "The last influence of a parent's legacy," By David Littlewood. Retrieved from http://www.newlifepublishing.co.uk/joyplus/leavingalegacy.htm.

[18] Ibid. See also Winship, A. E. *Jukes-Edwards—A Study in Education and Heredity.* Harrisburg, Pa., 1900.

[19] *Bartlett's Quotations.* Retrieved from http://www.bartleby.com/100/126.1.html.

[20] See http://www.idoodit.com/Story1945-1952.html.

[21] "Afraid to jump to safety, 2 children perish in fire," By John J. O'Brien, *Staten Island Advance,* December 11, 2005.

[22] "Nine Simple Filters," lecture by Brad Hays, July 14, 2006.

[23] Retrieved from http://www.quotationspage.com/quotes/Henry_Ford/.

[24] "Journalist Helen Thomas condemns Bush Administration," By Sarah H. Wright, *MIT Tech Talk,* November 6, 2002. Retrieved from http://web.mit.edu/newsoffice/2002/ thomas-1106.html.

25 Retrieved from http://www.hyperhistory.net/apwh/bios/
b4jelliot6ra.htm.

26 "Experts grappling with high suicide rate," By Mark Hansel, *Las Vegas Sun*, March 27, 2006. Retrieved from http://www.lasvegassun.com/sunbin/stories/sun/2006/mar/27/566616 691.html.

27 Major V. Gilbert in *The Last Crusade*, quoted in *Christ's Call To Discipleship*, J. M. Boice, Moody, 1986, p. 143.